May the God who is both great and good
make your marriage stronger and your hearts braver.
May He create not only a willingness to die for your
marriage but also a passion to live for it.

What people are saying about ...

TOGETHER

+ *"Together: Reclaiming Co-Leadership in Marriage* is simply the best book on marriage we have ever read—period. We highly and enthusiastically endorse it."

Dr. Che Ahn, president of Harvest International Ministry in Pasadena, California, **and Sue Ahn**

+ "In a time of societal drift, when the validity and the viability of marriage are under cultural attack, this book makes distinctive contributions. Instead of defining marriage as one of the constitutive institutions of society, the authors place it, more fundamentally, within the broad context of the nature of God, who is the original and eternal community of oneness. God, who is triune community in His intrinsic nature, loves community and lavishly gives community in the form of His image. He creates two as a community of oneness and commands them to fill the earth with more community. This book vividly describes the shape that marriage takes when it conforms to the creational intent of God for it. It is written with authenticity and enthusiasm. While its themes are grounded in Scripture, they are also steeped in the confirming evidence of lived-out experience. When so much confusion surrounds the theories and practices of marriage, even within Christian circles, this book provides an invaluable tool for individuals, couples, and groups to find their Scriptural bearings and receive real-life guidance for the proper conduct of the most fundamental of all relationships entrusted to humankind."

Dr. Gilbert Bilezikian, cofounder of Willow Creek Community Church and professor emeritus at Wheaton College in Wheaton, Illinois

+ "In a word, this message is a game changer. Once you catch the heart of God's co-leadership design for marriage, the effects will leak into every relationship you have. I'd go so far as to say that it isn't the position of God that gives Him power; it is the intense perfection of unity and oneness found in the Father, Son, and Holy Spirit relationship. This unity is what produced the universe and invites us to reflect and reveal His glory. As we co-lead together, we have seen so much beauty grow in our marriage and home as a direct result of our passionate pursuit of unity. God has poured His gold into Tim and Anne Evans, and we are the richer."

Jared Anderson, worship artist, Colorado Springs, Colorado, **and Megan Anderson**

+ "This book is a must-read for those who really want to be and stay married. Tim and Anne are true followers of Jesus, and together they have learned to follow the Beloved in tandem. When the Lord said of Adam, 'It is not good that the man live alone; I will make a helper suitable for him,' I have a serious hunch Tim and Anne were in His mind. Read this book and live it, and your marriage will be better."

Dr. Timothy Brown, president of Western Theological Seminary in Holland, Michigan

+ "The kingdom of God is about two very different worlds becoming one. Marriage is the greatest living example we have of this wonderful reality. Tim and Anne Evans are so very special to the kingdom of God and so very special to us. With a tremendous anointing as a spiritual Mom and Dad, their principles have helped shape our everyday lives. Through everything from the Traffic Light Principle to their push to live in the Larger Story, our marriage tool shed has been stocked up, and we are finding ourselves more in line with our good Father God's will. We love Tim and Anne. We trust them."

Jon Egan, worship pastor at New Life Church in Colorado Springs, Colorado, **and Paige Egan**

+ "There isn't a couple in the world I would rather hear talk on marriage than Tim and Anne Evans. Once you come into their home, the first thing you notice is the savory aroma of two people who not only are in love but have stayed in love. It's home cooking at its best. And it's so good you have to have the recipe. At last, they have put the recipe in print. Enjoy!"

Ken Gire, author of *Windows of the Soul* and
Intimate Moments with the Savior

+ "Tim and Anne Evans are delightful communicators, passionate about serving Christ, and devoted to equipping couples to serve God and each other without gender hierarchy. I pray for them as they write, teach, and advance the biblical basis for the shared authority and co-leadership of men and women, made one in Christ."

Dr. Mimi Haddad, president of Christians for Biblical Equality

+ "Tim and Anne have a profound message that is sure to challenge couples to walk in new Spirit-fueled unity. This book will awaken your imagination and shake you out of the tired old options of what it means to walk in oneness every day. How do we know? Because that's what their message has meant to us."

Glenn Packiam, campus pastor of New Life Downtown
in Colorado Springs, Colorado, **and Holly Packiam**

+ "Tim and Anne have written what they live and are living what they've written. Their life and message are one. We've watched them passionately live out co-leadership in marriage. We've seen God use them to rescue marriages—ours included. We encourage you to drink deeply from this life-giving book. Together revisit marriage 'in the beginning' ... your life and marriage will never be the same."

Morgan Snyder, teacher, speaker, and senior strategy
director at Ransomed Heart Ministries, **and Cherie Snyder**

+ "Marriage is under attack unlike ever before, and what this generation needs is a clearer understanding of God's heart and design. With a fresh and unique perspective, Tim and Anne help us reclaim everything marriage is supposed to be. Using practical stories from their own lives to illustrate biblical truths, this book is a message of hope that will help transform your marriage into everything God created it to be. By implementing the truths from *Together*, we've experienced firsthand the power and protection that comes from living out co-leadership unity principles."

John Stickl, lead pastor of Valley Creek Church
in Flower Mound, Texas, **and Colleen Stickl**

+ "Tim and Anne have captured fresh insights into biblical marriage that truly apply to real people in real marriages. Their approach doesn't aim to sugarcoat the challenges of marriage. Instead, they deliver sound teaching and inspiration through their revolutionary message on reclaiming co-leadership. Their creative, fun-to-read stories, coupled with practical, biblically sound principles, have blended into a book that is usable, stirring, and long overdue. Whether you are looking for hope in a hurting marriage or a new level of excellence in a good one, this is your next 'must-read!'"

Jack and Becky Sytsema, co-founders of
Children of Destiny in Holland, Michigan

+ "Marriage books often lead couples into a tug-of-war over headship-submission-authority or love and respect. Tim and Anne focus on the freedom found 'in the beginning.' In Genesis a husband and wife are invited to co-lead together and echo the plurality of God's Trinitarian nature. We've never heard a marriage message that challenges husbands and wives to walk together in mutual equality and mutual authority. Having hosted REAL LIFE marriage gatherings in our home, we've experienced the impact Tim and Anne's hearts and message have on marriages."

David Wilson, MD, and Haley Wilson, Colorado Springs

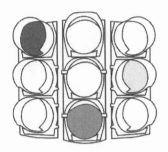

TOGETHER

Reclaiming **Co-Leadership** in Marriage

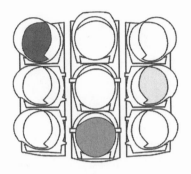

TOGETHER

Reclaiming **Co-Leadership** in Marriage

tim+anne evans

TOGETHER

Published by REAL LIFE Ministries

PO Box 6800, Colorado Springs, CO 80934

For ordering information visit Amazon.com

The stories in this book are based on decades of ministry, counseling, and real-life experiences. Names and details regarding some individuals whose stories are told in this book have been changed to protect their privacy. Editorial liberties have been taken to combine certain stories and circumstances for the purpose of clarity and illustration.

ISBN 978-0-9914-2880-9

Cover Design: Amy Konyndyk

Printed in the United States of America

First Edition 2014

DEDICATION

To God, the Author of marriage.

To our children, grandchildren, spiritual children, and future
family generations. We pray each of you are passionate
about God and His original marriage design.

To our Prayer Shield Team, who faithfully
love, encourage, and pray for us.

To men and women who have been spiritual fathers and mothers
to us. Your love and spiritual DNA are woven throughout this book.

To those who read this book and implement God's co-leadership
marriage principles. And to those who will build on what we have
written about gender equality and co-leadership in marriage.

We pray God builds a co-leadership marriage team,
a network of relationships united in heart about a
mission—God and marriage—that matters.

CONTENTS

INTRODUCTION

Hi. We are Tim and Anne Evans—or, as we like to say, "tim+anne," which we think visually represents the "togetherness" in our marriage.

For most of our lives together, we were a fireman and a nurse. Although we've moved beyond those roles now, we've retained our love of helping people who are hurting. But for all our married years—thirty-eight now— we've been husband and wife.

And we have to say, *we love marriage*! Truth be told, *we'd die for our marriage*.

But many couples we meet can't say that; sadly, if pressed they'd say *they're dying because of their marriage*. When we as a fireman and a nurse hear words like that, we know there's a crisis, an emergency, and something must be done. That's why we're writing this book. Are more marriage resources available today than ever before? Absolutely. But despite all the information out there, marriage is not doing well—not at all. There's a ton of information but little (if any) inspiration.

Here's the deal: we believe marriages are suffering because the marriages in our world today have strayed from God's original design.

We can already see the eyes rolling and hear someone say, "Oh, you want us to get back to some idyllic version of Mayberry, right?" No, we don't.

We want to point back further than Mayberry (or *Mad Men*, for that matter). A lot further. In this book we want to draw your attention to Eden, a place where a man and woman were unified in body, mind, soul, and spirit. Eden represents the incredibly unique reality of mutual equality and mutual authority in the marriage relationship—what we call *co-leadership*.

Now, we can see more eyes rolling and hear someone say, "C'mon, Paradise has been lost." And we would agree. While Scripture says that marriage is a good thing,[1] it also says that those who marry will face trouble in this life.[2] But just because that first Paradise was lost doesn't mean we can't revisit Eden and learn from God's original design—and then, with God's help, re-create that in our marriages today—*together*.

We love marriage. Ours is not perfect, and although we would die for our marriage, our hearts' desire is to live passionately for our marriage. And we long for you to feel that way about yours. It's not easy. There'll be trouble—and on some days, trouble with a capital T. But it's possible. If an old Chicago suburban fireman and his nurse bride can do it, so can you.

Together, we have experienced it. And together, you can too!

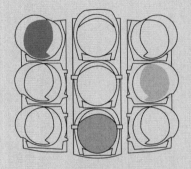

PART ONE

God's Co-Leadership Marriage Design

Haven't you read ... that at the beginning the Creator "made them male and female," and said, "For this reason a man will leave his father and mother and be united to his wife, and the two will become one flesh"? So they are no longer two, but one flesh. Therefore what God has joined *together,* let no one separate.

Matthew 19:4–6 NIV

CHAPTER 1

THE TRAFFIC LIGHT PRINCIPLE

Most of what I recall was the blood.

Request for the fire department, 1880 Bonnie Brae Lane, woman with gunshot to the head.

Adrenalin shot through my rookie fireman's veins as our team hustled into action. Our ambulance sped to the location. Dispatch crackled an update: *Be advised, gunshot victim's husband is in the apartment building. He is armed and dangerous! There are small children in the apartment. Stand by for police and proceed with extreme caution.*

As we arrived at the scene, a police officer's squad car screeched to a halt beside our ambulance. Together we took the elevator to the third floor, then ran down the hallway behind the officer, who had his .357 drawn.

We kicked in the apartment door and discovered a nightmare.

Blood everywhere. And three young children running, screaming, "Daddy shot Mommy! Daddy shot Mommy!" The officer ran through the apartment with gun held high, shouting for the husband.

It's difficult to describe how fast everything happened, yet the scene seemed to unfold in slow motion. Still, we had a job to do. We knelt beside the young wife, who lay in a pool of blood. We checked her ABCs (Airway, Breathing, Circulation) and quickly realized this young woman's life was about to end. We couldn't save her, so we focused on what little good we could do in the short time she had left.

Later, in the calm of my home, I struggled with my emotions.

I was a young fireman, husband, and new father, and I felt angry. I felt sad. *How could a husband shoot his wife in the head with his children watching?* I wondered. This young woman's life, all her potential—what a loss. I worried about her three children. What would their lives be like with a dead mom and a dad spending a lifetime in prison? I fought back tears as I thought about my own wife and newborn son.

As I held my emotions at bay and tried to process this emergency call, I couldn't help but wonder how things had gone so wrong for that couple. Surely their marriage had to have started out like most—passionate, devoted, hopeful. Surely in some fashion they had stood before family and friends and God and made promises to each other.

> *For better, for worse,*
> *for richer, for poorer,*
> *in good times and bad,*
> *in sickness and health,*
> *to love, honor, and cherish,*
> *till death do us part.*

Who would have predicted on that bright wedding day that things could have gotten so dark? What happened? When did this man and woman become something other than husband and wife? How did the dream of marriage turn into that nightmare?

While most couples never experience this level of violence, the reality is that countless husbands and wives are involved in a less dramatic but just as deadly kind of picture. Sticks and stones can break your bones, and negative words and cruel actions can break your heart into pieces, damaging both the spirit and the soul of a spouse, nurturing doubts that demand questions:

> Did I marry the wrong person?
> Why isn't our marriage as fulfilling as I'd hoped?
> How did we get so far from where we started?
> Where did we take a wrong turn?

Okay, here's the deal. We're guessing you've got some marriage problems right now. If everything was rosy, you probably wouldn't have picked up this book. In other words, you're in trouble, on some level, to some degree. There might not be a pool of blood on the floor ... but there might be a stream of tears on your cheeks. You may not even have the strength to finish this book. But we want to do what little good we can in the time you have.

We're going to get right to the vitals and give you some life-saving help. We want to give you the gold at the beginning. We're not going to insist you wade through chapter after chapter, building a foundation before we give you the practical advice. That's the progression of most books—you have to earn it. But we're going to be counterintuitive, working in what we believe to be the way of grace. We want to share with you this one way of relating as husband and wife that has revolutionized our marriage. It's something you can begin practicing right now.

Now, is there a foundation beneath what we're going to share? You bet. And our hope and prayer is that you will want to know what that is and will keep on reading, because it really is an amazing foundation. But as we said earlier, couples are in different seasons of marriage. You may need some immediate attention, and then you'll have the strength to gradually grow into the fullness of what we're talking about. The bottom line is that you don't have to jump to the end of the book to get the good stuff. It's right here in the beginning. We believe that once you get a taste of God's original co-leadership design for marriage, you will keep reading ... because the middle and end of our book have the good stuff too!

You need to know a couple things up front. First, you'll occasionally notice words or phrases in bold or italicized type. These terms are vitally important, but don't worry about them right now; we'll unpack their meanings a little later. Second, we have written a *Further Study* section at the back of the book where we provide you with additional information that is not included in the chapters.

Life Is Lived in a Story

anne

We hadn't been married long before we realized we both processed information and reached conclusions in different ways. Brilliant, aren't we? Tim tended to focus on the big picture and long-term effects of decisions, while I was concerned with immediate results. We were limited in our ability to process decisions in ways that brought *togetherness* to our marriage. At times disunity trumped unity. We felt as if we were wrestling together rather than working together. Both of us believed we were right. And we both wanted things our way.

As we thought about our decision-making process, one thing became obvious: most of the time we didn't include God. We wanted Him to be a part of our decisions, but on a practical level, we just didn't know what that looked like.

Then one day, while running errands, I found myself at a stoplight, waiting for the light to turn green. It dawned on me that every car in that intersection was directed by one small traffic light. The government had set up a system that protected all the drivers by helping us determine our next move. It's a simple system. Red means stop, yellow means slow, green means go. Age, gender, family of origin, position, and personal desires have nothing to do with the decision. Every driver is responsible to comply or face the consequences.

Can you imagine what would happen if the state left traffic decisions up to each individual driver? The driving handbook could read: "If you feel like stopping, stop. On the other hand, if you're in a hurry and have to get somewhere quickly, then go. Have it your way, because it's all about you!"

Or what if the manual read, "If you are in the mood to slow down and yield, go ahead. But if not, don't bother."

Or, "If a male and a female are approaching an intersection, the male has the right-of-way."

What if each driver responded to the color of the traffic light according to personal feelings and interpretations? For some drivers, red could mean go and green could mean stop.

What if you didn't like traffic lights? What if you didn't like to obey laws?

What if you believed that driving with the safety of others in mind was not as important as having it your way?

Imagine the chaos if all of us did things our way.

As I reflected on this simple approach to getting drivers to work together, I thought, *Why can't Tim and I set up a system that encourages unity in our marriage? Why can't we design a system to protect us from our natural desire to live life our way?*

When I got home, Tim and I spent some time discussing how a traffic-light system could benefit our marriage in terms of co-leading and making decisions together. Over time we devised the **Traffic Light Principle**. Here's how it works:

First, whenever we need to make a decision, we begin by individually *inquiring of the Lord*. The Bible is filled with stories of leaders—including

King David, Samuel, Solomon, the Israelites and many others—who were blessed when they inquired of the Lord. And when they failed to include God in their decision making process they ran into trouble.[1] In the New Testament men and women were encouraged to include God in decisions by asking Him for wisdom.[2] Throughout this book we will utilize the acronym—**I.O.T.L.**—to remind readers of the importance to *inquire of the Lord* and ask God for wisdom.

Practically, we **I.O.T.L.** and invite God into our decision-making process; in other words, we pray. We believe that this crucial step reaffirms our priority of focusing on God and listening to Him. Listening and waiting for God protects us from speeding ahead with our own agenda.

Individually we pray something like this: "Lord, speak to me in a language I can understand. Give me a red light if You are saying no. Give me a yellow light if You are saying wait. Give me a green light if You are saying go."

The second part of the **Traffic Light Principle** involves coming together after we pray and sharing what direction we sense the Lord is leading us. When we first began to test this principle, we had lots of questions: *What happens if we come together and don't have the same color light? What if one is green and the other is red?*

To address these issues while keeping our process simple, we agreed on the following guidelines:

> 1. We will proceed only if we are in unity. First, we **I.O.T.L.** *(inquire of the Lord),* if we do not have the same color light, we will agree to wait because for us *unity trumps disunity*.
> 2. If our lights remain different while we are waiting, we will continue to pray, listen, and discuss the decision. If appropriate, we will pull in a third party for insight, wisdom, and feedback.

3. We will keep waiting while regularly revisiting the decision until we both sense God giving us the same signal.

It's important to understand the key component in our **Traffic Light Principle** is that it includes *three* lights. The middle light represents what God is saying: "If any of you lacks wisdom, let him ask of God, who gives to all generously."[3] One light represents what the wife senses from God, and one light represents what the husband senses from God.

NAVIGATING A DIFFICULT ROAD TEST

As we put the **Traffic Light Principle** into action, we both agreed that being united did not mean we had to think exactly the same. We acknowledged our differences and were committed to celebrating them. We decided to focus on *unity trumping disunity* by being mutually submitted to God and to each other. We would not move ahead until we both agreed. We would resist the temptation to justify our positions, power up, or allow the stronger personality to make the final decision.

Having talked all these things through up front, we felt pretty good about our new plan. However, not long after we agreed to implement this principle, we realized that walking it out was not as easy as we first thought.

Life Is Lived in a Story

tim

I have loved motorcycles my entire life. Well, actually I *love* people—I *like* motorcycles. A lot. Growing up, my brothers and I always had motorcycles.

Now, I have never been the kind of person who has to have new things. I am just as happy with a used car as with a brand-new one. In fact, for most of our marriage I regularly purchased vehicles from firemen who took special care of their cars. I purchased three from my buddy Murph. He's the kind of guy who waxes under the hood of the engine. Rumor had it that he put a blanket over the entire car as he tucked it into the garage and kissed it good night! When Murph wanted to buy a new car, I got first dibs on his old one and encouraged him to buy a specific new color of car since I knew it would eventually be mine.

Dave Grant is another fireman friend who takes great care of his vehicles. He also loves motorcycles. When he wanted to purchase a brand-new 1981 Honda CB 750 Custom motorcycle with the stock Hondaline fairing, stereo, and all the options, I encouraged him to buy the two-tone blue (my favorite color). So Dave purchased my future motorcycle.

One day when I reported to the firehouse, Dave grabbed me. "Hey, Timmy, I'm selling my bike. Do you still want it?"

"Are you kidding me? I've been dreaming about that bike since I helped you pick it out." When he told me the price, I said, "Great."

Dave mentioned that three other firemen wanted him to skip me and sell it to them, but he'd told them, "No way. Timmy has been bugging me for this bike for years."

I couldn't wait to tell Anne I was getting my new bike—the one Dave had been keeping for me. The next morning I got off duty, went home, and told her the great news. Anne was excited for me. But then, as I was heading out the door to my side job, she casually said, "Hon, should we do the 'red-yellow-green light' thing we agreed to do when making decisions like this one?"

I said, "Sure, pray about it and let me know what your light is." Then I headed to work, totally confident that the bike was mine.

Seeing Red at a Yellow Light

That night after we put the kids to bed, Anne said, "Can we talk?"

"Sure. What's up?" I noticed she was in a somewhat serious mood.

"Tim, you are such a great provider for our family. I know there are very few things you really want. You are not the kind of husband who buys a lot of things or has a long toy list …"

"What's your point?"

"I know how long you have wanted Dave's motorcycle—"

Her words hit me like a Chicago Bears middle-linebacker blindside tackle. I immediately interrupted. "Anne, I have been riding motorcycles forever. I'm a safe driver, I wear a helmet, I don't drink and drive—"

She stopped me midsentence. "I know all that, Tim, and I agree with you on all those points. It's not any of that …"

"Then what?"

She hesitated, then softly said, "Remember our agreement to pray before making any major decisions? Well, I did that. The kids went down for a nap this afternoon. I got on my knees and asked God about the motorcycle, fully expecting to get a green light. But when I prayed, I sensed a yellow light. I thought to myself, *This can't be happening*. I know how much you have wanted Dave's bike. So I asked God again, and again I sensed a yellow light. I could not believe what I was seeing."

My mind kicked into rapid-fire power-up mode. "Hon, this can't be right! My green light is so green it's like I am on the Emerald Isle! Do you have any idea how many times I have bugged Dave to sell me this bike? I even helped him pick out the color when he bought it. Plus, I already told him yes. If it's the money, I am selling my old bike, and I have some money saved in my firehouse locker. Hon, do not tell me you don't have a green light."

"I'm sorry, I know how bad you want this bike. Hear me: I want you to have it too. I am sick about this. I wish I could tell you my light was green. But honestly, when I asked God, I kept sensing a yellow light."

"Whoaaa ... I have to think about this." I retreated to the garage, where my mind continued to race. *I can't believe this. What is Dave gonna think? Now Dick Munch will buy it.* I mentally grumbled, *Whose idea was this traffic-light thing anyway?* Then I had a new thought: *Wait a minute! What if I give Anne a free coupon that would be like a get-out-of-jail-free card next time she wants something? No, wait. I know ... I will agree with her and then secretly buy the motorcycle and keep it at the firehouse. When I want to ride it, I'll drive my old bike to the firehouse, leave it there, and take my new one for a ride. She'll never know. In a few months this will blow over, Anne will have a green light, and I will have my bike.*

The plan was genius. But that night the genius couldn't sleep. Conflicting thoughts flooded my mind. *Do I really want to lie to Anne? We did agree to implement this deal. On the other hand, she has no idea the razzing I will get if I back out after harassing Dave about "my" bike. What should I do?*

Then it hit me: *I'll call Dick Swetman. He is so close to God, he can ask Him to change her yellow light to green.*

The next day I phoned Dick, and we met at our usual place. Dick had been a spiritual mentor to me for a long time. Since I had called the meeting, I had to buy lunch. As we ate, I poured my heart out. I told him how I had picked out the color of this bike and stressed the fact that, if I didn't buy it, three other guys were lined up. I explained that we had the cash. Dick listened attentively as I outlined all the reasons why I should buy the bike, and then I wrapped up with the words, "Dick, this bike is mint—it has my name on it."

When I finished, he paused and looked me directly in the eyes. He said in his raspy voice, "Timmy, did you really ask God to give you a red-yellow-green light?"

"Well, sort of ..."

Then Dick said, "Maybe it would be a good idea to *really* ask God for a traffic light." Sensing my disappointment, he softly said, "Timmy, it's *only* a motorbike."

I thought, *What does he mean, "only a motorbike"? He didn't even say it right; it's called a motorcycle, not a motorbike!* But what I said was, "Dick, this thing is perfect. I have to get it. Can't you support me on this?"

He grabbed my shoulder and firmly said, "Timmy, have you *inquired of the Lord*?" Then he reminded me of the verse he had required me to memorize: "If any of you lacks wisdom, let him ask of God, who gives to all generously and without reproach."[4] He said, "Timmy, ask for God's wisdom and do what He says"—and then he walked out!

I thought, *Why do I bother with this guy? What does he know? He has probably never even ridden a "motorbike."* As I got up to pay the bill, another thought came to me: *I am actually paying for this guy's lunch … again! What did he tell me that was of any real value?*

Shifting into Reverse

On the way home I calmed down a bit. *Okay, Dick is a good guy. He loves Anne and me and our family.* Remembering his words, "Timmy, have you *inquired of the Lord*?" I pulled the car into Campanneli Park near our home and sat for a while. Finally I said, "Okay, God, do You have anything for me on this?" A minute or so passed, but it felt like an hour. Eventually, I put the car in reverse, impatiently thinking, *I have stuff to do.* Just then I sensed this message penetrating my brain: *Tim, this is not about the motorcycle.*

I responded, "What? That's crazy! This is *all* about the motorcycle. It's about making a deal with Dave years ago. It's about not having to borrow money. It's about one of the few things a hardworking guy like me enjoys!" I rambled on for a bit, and then I asked, "Okay, if this is not about the motorcycle, what is it about?"

A short pause, a soft answer: *This is all about you, Tim.*

"All about *me*? I don't ask for much. I work my tail off, I provide for my family ..." Suddenly I realized I was using the word *I* a lot. The question began to dog me: *Could this really be all about me?*

I sat in the car for a half hour, trying to overcome my inclination to go back to my plan to buy that motorcycle with or without a green light from Anne. I reviewed the facts of the situation. We both had agreed to do the traffic-light thing. I knew she wanted me to have the bike, and I definitely respected the way she heard from God. Okay, even Dick's counsel was probably right on. But ... I really wanted this bike. I'm not shittin' you—I *really*, *really* wanted it.

It was a moment of truth in my young heart and life. As I sat there, I thought about everything I did have and reviewed my list out loud: "I do have a great marriage, great kids, great friends. I love my job and our church. And I already have a motorcycle." As I reviewed the cards on my table, I realized that my plans were all about me. I knew in my gut what I had to do. I also knew that if I went home right then, I would probably try to guilt Anne into a pseudo-green light. So I headed directly to the firehouse, where I knew Dave was on duty.

I walked into the firehouse and found him cleaning my bike. "I've got it spotless for you, Timmy."

"Bud, can we talk?" We walked into the alley. I didn't quite know what to say. "Dave, you know how much I want your bike—"

"Timmy, if this is a cash problem, I can take payments."

"Thanks, no. It's ... well, you see ... Anne and I kinda made this deal where we would first pray about stuff ... and if we both didn't get a green light ... well, then ... we kinda said we would wait until ... we both got green lights."

Dave's response was blunt. "Let me get this straight: you are not going to buy the bike you helped me pick out, the one you have been harassing me about for years, because Annie doesn't have a green light?" Then he launched a missile that landed a direct hit to my heart. "Timmy, is this a Jesus thing?"

I nodded. "Yeah ... I guess it kinda is." Then I told him I had to get home.

He slapped me on the back and said jokingly, "Well, it's nice to see who wears the pants in your family."

Worn out, I headed home. As soon as I walked through the door, Anne could tell I was totally bummed. When I explained that I had stopped by the firehouse and told Dave no on the bike, she just looked at me in silence, her face as sad as I felt.

The next morning I walked into the firehouse to report for duty. I put my gear on the rig and went to open my locker. Pictures of traffic signals were taped all over it. The razzing started and never let up. That day the firehouse cook came up to me and said, "Hey, Timmy, I was thinking of having BLTs for lunch—that is, unless you don't have a 'green light.' Then I'll make burgers!"

The only highlight of the day was when I got a phone call. I immediately recognized Dick's soft raspy voice. "Timmy, Annie called me. She told me about the motorbike—" His voice cracked. "I'm really proud of you, son.

How about we meet for lunch tomorrow? I'll buy." I thanked him and hung up. At that point, even a free lunch sounded like a downer. The jokes continued as other firehouses got wind of the red-yellow-green-light deal. Let's just say it was one very l-o-n-g day.

The Turning Point

anne

I would like to add a brief note from my perspective.

What complicated the situation surrounding the motorcycle was the fact that both of us wanted to purchase Dave's bike. We had the money. I was excited to think of Tim purchasing something he would enjoy. I trusted him as a driver. Yet the Lord was clearly showing me yellow—*slow*—not green—*go*. I couldn't understand it.

Now, after being married over thirty-eight years and implementing this principle countless times, I realize that God is much more interested in *unity* than He is in either one of us getting our own way. God used the motorcycle as a turning point for us. It was the first time I recognized that Tim's response to my decision came out of his deep respect for me and my relationship with the Lord. Seeing him submit to God by submitting to what I was hearing encouraged me to look for ways to out-serve him. The fruit of our decision to include God cost us the bike, but we gained so much in trust, unity, and understanding togetherness. It was a crash course in co-leading, where *unity trumps disunity*. It was priceless.

But the story of the motorcycle wasn't over. I'll let Tim take it from here.

tim

That day at the firehouse was not the last chapter for me regarding Dave's bike. After I said no, another fireman named Dick Munch bought the bike and put lots of upgrades on it.

A few years later he called me and said, "Hey, Timmy, do you remember Dave's bike?"

After a long pause, I said, "Yeah, I seem to recall that."

"Well, it's just been sitting in my garage. I rode it for a while, then my wife got pregnant. Life happens, you know? Anyway, the bike hasn't been started for years. Any chance you'd be interested in buying it? That's, of course, if Annie has a 'green light.'"

I said, "Let me get back to you." Then I hung up the phone and said to Anne, "You're not going to believe this. Dave's bike is for sale again. What do you think?"

She said, "Tim, as you were talking to Dick and I realized it was about Dave's bike, I quickly *inquired of the Lord* and—I am not kidding—I immediately got a huge green light."

The only problem we could see was that, at the time, our finances were tight. I called Dick back and offered to get the bike out of his garage for five hundred dollars.

At first he just laughed and said he'd put that much into it after he bought it from Dave. Then he paused and said, "Oh, whatever. I just want to get rid of it. You can have it for five hundred dollars."

I couldn't believe it. I called a friend at the firehouse, Butch Adams, who owned a motorcycle shop. The next morning we loaded the bike onto his truck, brought it to his shop, bought a new battery, cleaned the carbs, and tuned it up. A few days later I was riding my bike.

This all happened over twenty-five years ago. And as I type this, that same old two-tone blue 1981 Honda CB 750 Custom motorcycle with the stock Hondaline fairing, stereo, and all the options is sitting in my garage. That bike represents so much more to me than just an old motorcycle. To this day, every time I throw my leg over it to go for a ride, I just smile and shake my head, thinking, *Only God would use a motorcycle to show me my true heart's desire, which centered not around a possession, but a Person.*

Over the years we have used the **Traffic Light Principle** for countless decisions: parenting issues, career changes, promotions, opportunities to move, vacations, purchases, even the choice to get a dog. We continue to find it a useful tool for co-leading together. Because the **Traffic Light Principle** is centered in prayer, listening to God, and mutually submitting to God and each other, this principle provides opportunities to die to selfishness.

Okay, there it is. We challenge you to implement the **Traffic Light Principle** and see how it transforms the decision-making process in your marriage. You can start this if you've been married two weeks or twenty-two years. It is not dependent on some high level of super-spirituality. All you need is willingness—in other words, just give it a try. We believe God will honor your desire to have a marriage worth passionately living for.

Remember: **I.O.T.L.** (*inquire of the Lord*) and *unity trumps disunity*. These are at the heart of walking out God's original co-leadership marriage design. Co-leading opens the door to other centered living where *marriage is not about me, but about we.*

It's probably some kind of literary suicide for a couple of authors to say, "You can put the book down and stop reading now—maybe sell it on eBay if you want." But we are saying that. You have enough right now to open up your marriage into something it hasn't been and something it can become. And if you choose to stop here, please hear us say *thank you.* But if you want to know a little more about what's behind this traffic-light thing and that unity stuff and what in the world co-leading means, then let's take the next step in our journey together.

CHAPTER 2

THE STARTING PLACE

God's Purpose—the *Why* of Marriage

Where you start determines where you end.

Life Is Lived in a Story

anne

Tim and I live in Colorado Springs, near the base of America's mountain—Pikes Peak. We decided last spring that we wanted to climb this mountain, all 14,115 feet of it. We knew disciplined training was crucial for success, so we hiked four or five times a week, gradually increasing our distance over the summer months. Finally the big day arrived, and we set out before sunrise. Since I am directionally challenged, Tim felt it would be a great confidence booster if I ran point on map reading and directions. I agreed, and so in the pitch-black parking lot I used my flashlight to read our directions:

From the parking lot you will see the beginning of the trailhead. Within a mile you will see a sign marking the 664A trail. Follow the 664A fork and continue up the trail on a gradual ascent. When you come to a log bridge, cross over and begin an aggressive ascent.

As I looked at the sign at the beginning of the trailhead, I was a little surprised it included only a few safety reminders for hikers. I guess I expected something more dramatic, like PIKES PEAK DEAD AHEAD! But I figured true mountaineers had no need for such displays, so we forged ahead, together. According to the directions I'd just read, we would reach our first landmark about a mile into the climb. But it's difficult to determine mileage when you're hiking in the dark. When we didn't pass the 664A sign, I was a little concerned. I remember turning to Tim and saying, "We must have missed the sign, but that looks like the log bridge just ahead." So we forged ahead, together.

As the sun rose, the view was absolutely breathtaking. The sky was clear and the air was crisp; it could not have been a more perfect day. I checked our directions once again:

Continue up the trail as you prepare to begin an aggressive ascent above tree line. Look for the area marked Devil's Playground. At this point the summit will be in full view.

I definitely would not have described the next section as *aggressive*, but instead of stopping to check the map, I ignored my uncertainty, thinking, *We're in better shape than I thought!* But as the miles passed, I kept wondering why we had not reached tree line yet—and then there was this mountain parallel to us that sure looked like Pikes Peak. Well, I'm sure you can tell where this story is going. Tim and I were on the wrong mountain, mainly because we had started from the wrong parking lot, a few hundred feet from the correct trailhead. The hike we had trained for and anticipated all summer ended up a disaster.

Our mountain misadventure reflects the experience of many couples who set out to enjoy the adventure of marriage. Oftentimes, preparations are made: going to premarital counseling, getting advice from family and friends, reading books, attending conferences, all in hopes of finding the roadmap to marital bliss. But life rarely looks like what we expect, and it's dangerously easy for couples to lose their way, ignore warning signs (which are sometimes in their gut), and hold on to a pride that keeps them from asking for help. Then, in a true crisis moment, they convince themselves they'll find their way if they just keep going ... only to find themselves utterly lost.

WHERE YOU START DETERMINES WHERE YOU END

So here's a question: where did *your* marriage start? Not the address of the church where you exchanged vows or the name of the town where you and your spouse stood before a justice of the peace, but what *map* guided it? In other words, what examples of marriage did you have to go by? These could have been positive (your grandparents were married for fifty years) or negative (a friend's parents divorced when their nest emptied out) or just sorta blah (your parents stayed together but lived essentially separate lives). Whether we're aware of it or not, the examples around us become the map that guides us through the peaks, valleys, and plateaus of *togetherness*.

We'd like to invite you to go back with us to where it all started, and by *all* we mean *everything*. We believe it's the correct map—not the only one, mind you, but the correct one. We are unapologetically followers of Christ, so we're going back to the book of Genesis. And as we get started, you may feel like you're hiking in the predawn dark, but hang in there; it'll become clearer. This map gets started *in the beginning* ...

IN THE BEGINNING

> In the beginning *God* created the heavens and the earth. Now the earth was formless and empty, darkness was over the surface of the deep, and the *Spirit of God* was hovering over the waters. And God *said*...[1]

In just three short verses, God revealed some amazing truths about His identity. But you might miss them if you're not looking for the landmarks. We italicized the words in that passage we'd like you to especially notice:

> *God*
> *Spirit of God*
> *said*

Have you ever heard the phrase *the Trinity*? As in, God the Father, God the Son, God the Holy Spirit? Well, guess what? Here, no further than three verses into the first book of the Bible, we find the three distinct persons of the Godhead. Genesis 1:1 introduces God the Father, but He was not alone. Verse 2 introduces the Spirit of God. Most people think of the Holy Spirit as a New Testament ghost-like character who arrived on the scene only after Jesus returned to the Father, but right there in the beginning the Holy Spirit's presence was "hovering over the waters."[2] And at the start of verse 3, another person of the Trinity of God is introduced. The text reads, "God *said*."

Now this one's not so clear, so we've got to look closely. The gospel of John refers to Jesus Christ as the Word and confirms His presence at creation: "In the beginning was the *Word*, and the *Word* was with God, and the *Word* was God. He was in the beginning with God."[3] The Bible continues, "And the *Word* became flesh, and dwelt among us, and we saw His glory, glory as of the only begotten from the Father, full of grace and truth."[4] The apostle Paul also wrote about the *Word*—Logos—Jesus Christ:

> He is the image of the invisible God, the firstborn of all creation. For by Him all things were created, both in the heavens and on earth, visible and invisible, whether thrones or dominions or rulers or authorities—all things have been created by Him and for Him.[5]

Jesus became "flesh," which means "human." He is first introduced as a human—and secondarily as a male. From the very beginning, we see *the Trinity*: God the Father, God the Holy Spirit, and God the Son.

Of all the ways that God could have begun His story, why this way? Could He have been pointing to something significant about His nature that He wanted every person to know? Yes! From the very beginning, God declared Himself a *we* instead of a *me*: a picture of community and perfect oneness. There's no indication of hierarchy, headship, a designated leader, or subordination within the Trinity of God. Now, hold that thought.

REFLECTING AND REVEALING THE IMAGE OF GOD

You're probably wondering what all this has to do with marriage, right? The answer is *everything*.

Just after we meet the triune God in the first verses of Genesis, we witness the miracle of creation. God called into existence light and darkness; the heavens and seas; land, plants, and trees; sun, moon, and stars; birds and fish; and all the animals.

Let's look at the words God spoke next, again noting in particular the italicized landmark words:

> Let *Us* [God the Father + God the Son + God the Holy Spirit] make *man* [humankind: male and female] in *Our* image [God the Father + God the Son + God the Holy Spirit], according to *Our* [God the Father + God the Son + God the Holy Spirit] likeness.[6]

This Trinitarian God, who is the essence of community, created *more* community—humankind (male and female)—in His image and likeness. Image is defined as "a person or thing bearing a close likeness to somebody or someone else"[7] and likeness is defined as "a representation of somebody or something."[8] Remember *both* man and woman were within the first created human: the man. The man was formed out of dust, and the woman was fashioned out of the man. Both man and woman were made in God's image, intrinsically equal as created human beings.[9]

Reviewing the creation account, notice how God repeatedly referred to Himself in the plural with the words *us* and *our*. This is significant because the *we* instead of *me* in the Trinity of God directly relates to His design and purposes for marriage: "God created man *in His own image*, in the image of God He created him; male and female He created *them*."[10] Since God created man *and* woman in His image, marriage invites a husband and wife to represent God's nature in a unique and remarkable way.

Traditionally, people refer to God as "He." And in the church, God is typically portrayed as being more masculine than feminine. However, God is neither male nor female. He is not a human being; His essence transcends sexuality. God is not a man, we read in Hosea 11:9 and Numbers 23:19. These texts emphasize the difference between deity and humanity. However, God's image includes *both* masculine and feminine characteristics. God created humans in His image with both masculine and feminine characteristics to **reflect** and **reveal** the diversity and plurality within His nature.

Some biblical texts tend to focus on the more stereotypical masculine characteristics of God; for example Exodus 15:3 says, "The LORD is a warrior; the LORD is His name." And other biblical texts tend to focus on the more stereotypical feminine comforting and merciful characteristics of God; for example, "blessed be the God and Father of our Lord Jesus Christ, the Father of mercies and God of all comfort, who comforts us in our affliction so that we will be able to comfort those who are in any affliction with which we ourselves are comforted by God."[11]

Reflecting specifically on masculinity and femininity, we believe that there is no man who ever lived who was more of a man than Jesus Christ. Yet there is only one time in the Bible where Jesus described Himself. In Matthew 11:29, He said: "I am *gentle* and *humble* in heart." If we look at our culture, gentleness and humility are *not* typical words used to describe a man.

Another example of this dual masculine and feminine nature is the apostle Paul. He was a man's man in every sense, he totally gave his life for Christ, and he authored much of the New Testament. And Paul also understood the masculine and feminine aspects of being made in God's image. As he wrote to Timothy, his spiritual son, "We proved to be gentle among you, as a nursing mother tenderly cares for her own children. Having so fond an affection for you, we were well-pleased to impart to you not only the gospel of God but also our own lives because you had become very dear to us."[12]

All this is to say, since God's essence includes both masculine and feminine characteristics, it makes us wonder—*what is the most accurate way to describe God?* The Bible answers that question: "God is love."[13] It's important to remember that love is not exclusive to masculinity or femininity or based on gender.

Each and every person of the Trinity (Father-Son-Spirit) models love in equality and mutuality. We see no evidence of a pecking order or hierarchy. We do not see one person of the Trinity as the head, having authority, the leader over other parts of our Trinitarian God. God cannot be inferior to God.

Furthermore, there is nothing in the creation account that implies any differences in God's image in the man or woman. The man and woman are mutually equal as created beings who are *both* made in the image of God the Father, God the Holy Spirit, and God the Son.[14]

Bottom line for us is that the essence in the tri-unity of God is a mystery humankind will never fully comprehend. Likewise, the essence of marriage in "two becoming one" is a mystery humankind will never fully comprehend.

THE *WHY* OF MARRIAGE

Back to the creation story. It's important to note that before God created man and woman, He explained *why*. God said, "And let *them* [male and female] rule over ... the birds ... cattle ... [and] every creeping thing."[15] Before God created humans He explained their mission and purpose. God created both man and woman in His image to exercise dominion (**rule**) as husband and wife—*together*.

Co-leadership (exercising dominion together) is at the heart of God's mission and purpose for marriage. It's important to remember that God gave authority and dominion to *both* the man and the woman. In God's original marriage design the husband and wife lived in oneness (both made in the image of God) and purpose (both given the procreation and dominion mandates). In Eden, before sin entered the story, the man and woman became one in spirit, soul, and body.

Yes, it's apparent that God made a big deal about equality and co-leadership in marriage. Therefore, let's break down aspects of the Genesis creation story verse by verse. After creating numerous things that were *not* made in His image, God described His plan to create beings made in His image, according to His likeness:

> Genesis 1:26—"Let *Us* make man [humankind] in *Our* image, according to *Our* likeness."

> Genesis 1:26b—God explained the mission and purpose for the beings He was about to create: "And let *them* rule over the fish ... birds ... cattle ... [and] every creeping thing." The new beings God created would have authority, and *together* they would co-lead and exercise shared rulership (dominion).

> Genesis 1:27—God created humans: "God created man [humankind] in His own image, in the image of God He created him; *male* and *female* He created *them*." God created *both* male and female in His Trinitarian image.

After God created man and woman He did a number of things:

> Genesis 1:28—"God blessed *them.*" The heart of a good God is to
> bless. Think about this: of all the things God could have done after
> creating humans, the first thing He did was bless them. Notice that
> God blessed *both* the man and the woman.

Not only did God bless them, He gave good gifts to His children. God is
utterly good; His desire from the first breath of the first human beings—
before they *did* anything for Him—was to bless them. Both of them.

> Genesis 1:28b—God said to *both* the man and woman, "Be fruitful
> and multiply and fill the earth." This is the first mandate God
> gave to His children. He commanded the first married couple
> to bear children—to multiply and fill the earth. This is called the
> procreation mandate. First God blessed His children, then He
> commanded them to live fruitful lives and create more children,
> which would enable them to extend community and exercise
> dominion throughout the earth.

What an awesome story! The community within the Godhead created
more community—one man and one woman to **reflect** and **reveal** God's
Trinitarian nature. Then the Trinitarian God commanded the couple to
reproduce more community: "Be fruitful and multiply."[16] Again, note that
the procreation mandate was given to *both* the man and woman. They
were *both* given mutual authority and responsibility to co-lead together
and fulfill the dominion and procreation mandates.

> Genesis 1:28c—Next God repeated what He said before He
> created humans, instructing the man and woman to "rule over
> the fish of the sea and over the birds of the sky and over every
> living thing that moves on the earth." This is called the dominion/
> **rulership** mandate. Again, notice that this command was given

twice; once before God created humans, and again after He created the first married couple.

Genesis 1:29–30—God created, blessed, and commissioned *both* the man and woman, and He also gave good gifts to His children: "Behold, I have given you every plant yielding seed ... and every tree ... [and] every beast ... [and] every bird ... and every thing that moves on the earth." Again, God gave these gifts to *both* the man and woman.

Genesis 1:31—Throughout the creation story, after God created something, He declared it "good." However, the only thing God declared "not good" was man being alone. So God created woman—a helper (*ezer*)—to rescue man from his "not good" situation. After woman was created, God declared for the first time everything He created "very good".

Genesis 2:2—On the seventh day, God completed His work and rested—not because He was tired; but to give humankind a model for living a Sabbath lifestyle. This makes us wonder—*why did God create everything before He created humans?* This is only speculation, but maybe God did not want His children to see Him "doing" things. Instead He wanted them to experience Him for the first time not as God the Creator but as a good God. God is in essence good, and the heart of every good parent is to bless his or her children. So He prepared for His children a perfect environment as the context and support for their lives.

Genesis 2:3—God blessed and sanctified the seventh day. We envision God soaking in all the "very good" things He created; after rest came blessing.

When we think about God's design for marriage, we wonder: if, as some people believe, male leadership, hierarchy, headship, and female subordination are important to God and intrinsic in His design for maleness, femaleness, and marriage, don't you think God would have made setting the gender record straight a top priority from the very beginning? Being a God of order, wouldn't He have clearly designated a hierarchy and chain of command with God first, the husband second, and the wife third?

But the first thing God did after creating man and woman was to bless them. He blessed *both* the man and woman. Next God gave the procreation mandate (**reproduce**): "Be fruitful ... multiply ... fill the earth, and subdue it."[17] Then God gave the dominion mandate: "**Rule** over the fish ... birds ... [and] every living thing that moves on the earth."[18] God gave the procreation and dominion mandates to *both* the man and the woman. Together they enjoyed co-leadership in oneness and purpose.

If God's original plan for man and woman included a hierarchy, headship, or the husband having any measure of authority over his wife, He never mentioned it after creating the first couple. Nevertheless, after creating man and woman, God described the first bride and groom in a very unique way: they were "naked and ... not ashamed."[19] Keep that in mind. We will discuss that later.

Life Is Lived in a Story

tim

I served for over twenty years in a busy Chicago suburban fire department in Schaumburg, Illinois. Throughout my career I was blessed with a number of promotions (lieutenant, captain, battalion chief, and I retired second-in-command as deputy fire chief). As I advanced in my profession, I was privileged to be involved in a number of fire-officer training courses and certifications. In one particular leadership course our instructor asked, "What is the mission of your fire department?" Even with my many years in the department, and as a chief fire officer, I had no idea what our mission was—or if we even had a mission.

I met with our fire chief and asked him what our mission was. He blankly stared at me and said, "I have no idea." We took out the village manual and came across three to four pages that described our department and listed many of its responsibilities and functions. Our meeting ended with the chief challenging me, "Tim, why don't you work on rewriting our department's mission?"

I eagerly took the chief's challenge, and in the next month I visited fire-houses to ask our officers and firefighters for input on writing a new mission. Of course, some of them joked, "Chief, how about making our mission, 'We put the wet stuff on the red stuff'?"

As we seriously thought about our mission, we wanted it to capture what we were all about, and we wanted it to be simple enough for every member to be able to memorize. We decided on a three-word mission statement: "Service-Safety-Teamwork" (SST). These words captured the big picture of what we were all about: we were a **s**ervice organization; **s**afety would always be a top priority; and **t**eamwork is essential to accomplish any firefighting task. Our officers and firefighters were required to memorize our mission, and I even began to sign my memos with "SST."

THE 4-R *WHY* OF MARRIAGE

We believe that understanding the *why* of something helps a person more passionately live it out. For example, in the parent-child relationship, children are commanded to honor their parents. *Why?* "So it may go well with [them]."[20]

GOD'S MISSION FOR MARRIAGE

What about marriage? What is God's purpose for marriage? Following the example of the fire department's "SST" mission, we will utilize a simple acronym throughout this book. God's original design—His marriage mission—is for *both* the husband and wife to:

> **Reflect and Reveal**: God's plurality and nature; mutual equality; *both* made in God's image
>
> **Rule**: co-lead *together*; mutual authority; *both* given the dominion (rulership) mandate
>
> **Reproduce**: be fruitful and multiply; *both* given the procreation mandate

In the beginning ... In God's original marriage design, the first married couple celebrated marital oneness as they co-led in mutual equality and mutual authority. *Together* the husband and wife were commanded to extend their God-given dominion throughout the earth by living out what we refer to as the marriage **4 R's** (**reflect**, **reveal**, **rule**, **reproduce**).

In our experience, people typically approach mission from a perspective of outcome: things a person or couple plans to do or achieve. But in marriage the mission is not so much outcome but relationship, as a couple focuses first of all on God and second on each other.

CHAPTER 3

FROM *GOOD* ... TO *NOT GOOD* ... TO *VERY GOOD*

We finished the last chapter by saying that marriage is all about relationship, and it is. But if we asked ten people to define *relationship*, we'd no doubt get ten different answers. To get a clearer understanding of the word, let's go to where it all got started: the book of Genesis, the same place we explored in the last chapter. In the beginning, everything starts out good, then we find out something was missing—and then, well, it gets *really* good!

The Bible contains two accounts of creation in Genesis.[1]

Chapter 1 describes a big-picture overview, and chapter 2 describes a more intimate view. Let's return to the story: "Then the LORD God formed man of dust from the ground, and breathed into his nostrils the breath of life; and man became a living being."[2]

Up to this point God *spoke* everything into existence. But when God created a being made in His image, He changed His style of creating and got more intimately involved. Can you imagine the first encounter between man and his Maker? The God of the universe, the great I AM, took a hands-on approach when creating man. God's relationship with man was up close and personal. It has been that way from the beginning.

After God breathed life into man, He "took the man and put him into the garden of Eden to cultivate it and keep it."[3] And all this was good.

FROM "GOOD" TO "NOT GOOD"

Could life have been any better? God created man; He blessed him and gave him gifts; He related to him and gave him instructions for life. Man lived in a sin-free environment, surrounded by every imaginable beauty in the garden. Imagine this, guys. *The weather was perfect, the fish were always biting, food was plentiful, you didn't need to wear clothes, and working the garden was the kind of work that makes your heart and muscles feel strong and alive.* Sounds like paradise, huh?

However, in dramatic fashion God demonstrated an immeasurable depth to His character and humility. For the first time in recorded history, our good God declared that something about creation was not good. God said, "It is *not good* for the man to be alone."[4]

Which begs the question ... *why*?

Because God wanted more for man. God wanted man to identify with the part of His nature that longed to create. God wanted man to be fruitful and multiply, to fill the earth, to exercise dominion and **rule**. But He realized something was missing—or better yet, some*one*.

So how did God respond to man's "not good" situation? God declared, "I will make a helper suitable for him."[5] God chose a powerful word for the crown of creation: *helper* (*ezer* in Hebrew). That word describes the one He created to remedy man's "not good" situation.

Let's explore this word. *Ezer* is often translated as "helper" or "helpmeet." Unfortunately in our culture, *ezer* is often inaccurately defined as a wife being in a position inferior to that of her husband, which leads to the unbiblical conclusion that a hierarchy existed before the fall. But nowhere in the Genesis story of creation is the husband given any measure of authority over his wife—his helper.

As Dr. Gilbert Bilezikian noted,

> Adam's plight was that while he remained alone, he was only half the story. The image of God in him, itself the imprint of the nature of God, yearned for the presence of a counterpart without whom there could be no community and therefore no fulfillment of God's design. The image of God on earth could only reflect the reality of the Triune God in heaven through plurality of persons....
>
> Eve was created precisely to "help" him become with her the community of oneness that God intended for both of them to be together. To wrench the word *helper* from this precise context, where it has the strength of *rescuer*, and to invest it with the connotations of domesticity or female subservience violates the intent of the biblical passage.[6]

We also like what Carolyn Custis James had to say:

> Descriptions of women as dependent, needy, vulnerable, deferential, helpless, leaderless, or weak are—to put it

simply—wrong. Such definitions betray cultural biases and I fear a deep-seated misogyny. The *ezer* is a warrior. Like the man, she is also God's creative masterpiece—a work of genius and a marvel to behold—for she is fearfully and wonderfully made. The *ezer* never sheds her image-bearer identity. Not here. Not ever. God defines who she is and how she is to live in his world. That never changes. The image-bearer responsibilities to reflect God to the world and to rule and subdue on his behalf still rest on her shoulders too.

God didn't create the woman to bring half herself to his global commission or to minimize herself when the man is around. The fanfare over her is overblown if God was only planning for her to do for the man things he was perfectly capable of doing for himself or didn't even need. The man won't starve without her. In the garden, he really doesn't need someone to do laundry, pick up after him, or manage his home. If Adam must think, decide, pro-tect, and provide for the woman, she actually becomes a burden to him—not much help when you think about it. The kind of help the man needs demands full deployment of her strength, her gifts, and the best she has to offer. His life will change for the better because of what she contributes to his life. Together they will daily prove in countless and surprising ways that two are always better than one.[7]

Life Is Lived in a Story

tim

As a fire chief at major fires, I served as the incident commander. My responsibilities included overseeing the big-picture operations. I wasn't concerned with locating, confining, and extinguishing the fire—that's what the engine company was responsible for. I wasn't concerned with forcible entry, search and rescue, or ventilation—that's what the truck company was responsible for. I wasn't concerned with salvage, overhaul, and general cleanup—that's what the squad company was responsible for.

As fire chief I managed the overall fire scene. This included fire tactics, strategy, and safety. For example, I would make the decision about whether the fire would become an "extra alarm" fire, I established a Rapid Intervention Team (RIT) in case an unforeseeable emergency occurred, and I monitored multiple fire companies' progress. In the back of my mind I was always thinking about additional emergency calls we could be required to respond to while we were on the scene fighting this fire. I also knew that when the fire was under control, I would have to make more important decisions: things like prioritizing placing companies back in service, investigating fires, filing incident reports, and handling the media.

Nevertheless, there were occasions on the scene in which a firefighter would exit the building and say, "Chief, we need more hose; help me drag this charged hose line into the building." This fireman was in a "not good" situation and requested "help," and I responded as his "helper." Taking the role of helper to assist a firefighter who needed help was a no-brainer for me as the fire chief. It had absolutely nothing to do with authority. This firefighter could not advance a charged hose line into the building by himself. Therefore, as a helper I rescued him from his "not good" situation, and together we accomplished the necessary task.

Thankfully the men and women of the fire service work together as a team, helping one another put out fires and handle many "not good" situations. In addition, firefighters understand they have a common enemy. Therefore, they focus on unity (brotherhood and sisterhood) within the department and celebrate diversity in regard to other departments (rural, volunteer, paid on-call, suburban, and big-city fire departments).

Often in the church world, people endlessly argue about terms like *ezer*, which results in adding fuel to both church and relational fires. This results in many "not good" situations as people with different marriage views treat one another as enemies. Unfortunately, this leads to disunity and judging rather than celebrating the diversity in different marriage views and preferences.

Let's review. Before sin entered the story, the man and woman were equal. They *both* were made in the image of God. The man and woman were *both* given the procreation mandate: to be fruitful and multiply. And they were *both* given the dominion mandate: to **rule** together. God gave these mandates to *both* the man and the woman. Working together in mutual equality and mutual authority, the man and woman co-led in carrying out God's mission and mandates for marriage.

We encourage married readers to revisit God's original marriage design. Our sense is that you will quickly realize God created you and your spouse as equal partners. Equality is an intrinsic component within the Trinity of God; equality is also an intrinsic component in a Christian marriage.[8]

FROM "NOT GOOD" TO "VERY GOOD"

> So the LORD God caused a deep sleep to fall upon the
> man, and he slept; then He took one of his ribs and closed

up the flesh at that place. The LORD God *fashioned* into a *woman* the rib which He had taken from the man, and brought her to the man.[9]

Note that *woman* was God's designation of the female being He created. The Bible says God *formed* man[10] and *fashioned* woman.[11] Forming reminds us of a construction term. Forms are laid when a concrete foundation is poured. Fashioning reminds us of an artist creating a beautiful, priceless piece of art.[12]

How did man respond to God's solution to his "not good" condition of aloneness? When God presented the woman, the man said: "This is now bone of my bones, and flesh of my flesh; she shall be called *Woman*."[13] Remember, *woman* was God's designation in the preceding verse: "Bone of my bones and flesh of my flesh" relates to mutuality and kinship, not inequality, hierarchy, or female subordination. This statement regarding marriage provides a glimpse of the miracle and mystery of the *together-ness* in a husband and wife becoming one.

God created and named man, and He created and named woman. The man recognized the uniqueness of this new created being. Then God said, "*For this cause* a man shall leave his father and mother, and shall cleave to his wife; and the two shall become one flesh."[14]

Okay, quick review. Instead of God speaking humankind into existence, He created man out of dust and breathed life into him with the intimacy of a kiss. Then God declared the "not good-ness" of man being alone. So out of the solitary man, God fashioned another human being (*woman*), who was also made in God's image. Then God said *for this cause* a man shall leave, cleave, and become one flesh. Makes us wonder ... *could the cause God is referring to relate to the miracle and mystery, the unique together-ness in marriage of two becoming one?*

Leaving, cleaving, and becoming one flesh is a process exclusive to mar-riage. Leaving and cleaving precedes becoming one flesh: one man and one woman joining together in spirit, soul, and body. Notice the command is to "the two"—not just to the man or just to the woman; rather "the two" shall become one flesh. Becoming one flesh is a two-part process that involves the man becoming one with the woman as he enters her and the woman becoming one with the man as she receives him. The man deposits his life-giving seed into the woman's body, and God enables them to miraculously create more males and females who are also made in His image.

A husband and wife procreating within the context of marriage is God's provision for societies to continue from generation to generation. It's important to note that having children includes being both a biological and a spiritual parent. The apostle Paul had no biological children that we know of, but he had many spiritual children.[15] And the apostle John said this about his spiritual children: "I have no greater joy than this, to hear of my children walking in the truth."[16]

The last verse in Genesis 2 says: "And the man and his wife were both naked and were not ashamed."[17] 'Naked and not ashamed' was God's description of the first married couple. The man and woman were in rela-tionship with God and each other. There was no shame, blame, fear, or control. In Eden the husband was never designated as the leader, head, or spiritual cover over his wife. In God's original marriage design, *together-ness* prevailed. The husband and wife celebrated mutual equality (both made in the image of God) and *co-leadership* in mutual authority (both given the procreation and dominion mandates).

Here's a poetic version of celebrating nakedness without shame that will make you smile:

We speak of the fall, and I think he did
that man born a man and never a kid.
He tended the garden according to plan,
but lonely was he, this overalled man....

So one weary day he left barrow and tool,
took off his gloves and lay down in the cool.
Then God dreamed a keeper, not fish or a stone,
but flesh of man's flesh, bone of man's bone.
Sharp pain in his side woke the prince from his nap,
he stretched perfect limbs and adjusted his cap.

For a fella at naming it seemed since day one,
he stood before Eve twitterpated and dumb.
She grinned with the evening's dew still on her lips,
then clavicles, breasts, and mercy those hips.
Shucks, Lord, if she's not the fairest of all.
God smiled on creation's most beautiful fall.[18]

God's Original Marriage Design

God
Man and woman (co-leadership)
Nature

God's original design—the *why* of marriage—is for *both* the husband and wife to:

> **Reflect and Reveal**: God's plurality and nature; mutual equality; *both* made in God's image
>
> **Rule**: co-lead *together*; mutual authority; *both* given the dominion (rulership) mandate
>
> **Reproduce**: be fruitful and multiply; *both* given the procreation mandate

GOD'S "VERY GOOD" DESIGN FOR MARRIAGE

God created everything—light, waters, vegetation, plants, trees, living creatures, birds, cattle—and He declared each one good. However, after God created the first marriage, He declared all that He created was *very good*. Apparently, a good marriage did not accurately describe the very good of marriage. When it comes to marriage, might God be saying that good is not good enough?

God's "very good" design for a Christian marriage "in the beginning"[19] included two nonnegotiable components:

> 1. One man and one woman. God created humankind in His image—"*male* and *female* He created them."[20] Therefore, any marital relationship apart from one man and one woman goes against God's original marriage design.
> 2. Both husband and wife are in a personal relationship with God. Oneness (spirit-soul-body) and relationship with God are critical elements in a Christian marriage. If either the husband or the wife is not in a relationship with God, they cannot **reflect** and **reveal** the plurality in whose image they are created.

Reviewing the first marriage, we wonder: *could God be telling us something significant about Himself?* Namely, that He is a plurality who exists in community? He created humankind—men and women—to model the community intrinsic in His triune relational nature.

Relationship is at the heart of God and the heart of marriage. A man alone could not fully **reflect** and **reveal** the plurality of God. Man needed to be partnered with someone *after his kind*: another human being—a woman—with whom he could become one and create more human beings (men and women) made in God's image. God could have created many different relationships to begin humankind. He did not choose a family, a church, a town, or a village to **reflect** and **reveal** His image. Instead, He chose one man and one woman—*together*.

REAL LIFE MARRIAGE MOTTOS

REAL LIFE ministries has a number of marriage mottos. The first is **I.O.T.L.** (*inquire of the Lord*). The wisest thing a couple can do is to always include God and ask Him for wisdom. A second motto is *unity trumps disunity*, which refers to the togetherness and co-leadership that God designed for marriage. Another motto is *marriage is not about me*. This invites a question: *if marriage is not about me, then who is it about?*

A Christian marriage involves God. Every husband and every wife are called to live out the miracle and mystery of marriage in relationship with God the Holy Spirit, God the Son, and God the Father. Marriage invites a person to step out of the smaller story where self is the main character and *it's all about me* and into the Larger Story where God is the main character and *it's not about me*.[21] This becomes the pathway to advancing in intimacy with God, as well as to *co-leading together* and advancing in spirit, soul, and body oneness with a spouse.

Before we move on, we want to pause and address two groups of people: first, readers who are married to unbelievers and second, unmarried readers.

To followers of Christ who are married to unbelievers: our experience is this situation provides many opportunities for the believing spouse to live life in the Larger Story. We encourage the believing spouse to humbly **reflect** and **reveal** God to the unbelieving wife or husband. The way a believing spouse treats an unbelieving spouse tells a powerful story about the Person he or she is following. We encourage every believing spouse to continue to pray that his or her spouse's heart will be open to Jesus and His story. Remember, there is power in the gospel. [22] Keep in mind that sharing the life of Jesus is not about convincing or converting anyone. It is all about sharing His story: His love, birth, life, death, and life-giving resurrection.

Whether or not your spouse shares your faith, the best way to invite your spouse into the Larger Story is to live your life the same way Jesus did: in the context of love and relationship. We encourage you to avoid any unrighteous judging and to grow in loving God and loving the way He loves.

To unmarried readers: we want to be sure to point out to singles that fulfillment of God's purposes in life is not only available in marriage—"To the contrary, the Bible teaches that believers who can manage singleness find greater fulfillment in lives of celibate service than if they were married."[23]

However, for those of us who are married, the privilege and responsibility of living out the miracle and mystery of two becoming one—*co-leading together*—can utterly transform our approach to marriage and advance God's kingdom.

CHAPTER 4

CO-LEADERSHIP LOST

Life Is Lived in a Story

anne

Sue made an appointment with me to discuss some areas of concern in her marriage—in particular, her nearly nonexistent sex life with her husband.

As we talked about her family of origin, Sue admitted that she experienced intense feelings of rejection throughout her growing-up years. The pain from her childhood had never been resolved. Now it was affecting her marriage because she interpreted her husband's passive style of relating as another form of rejection.

To complicate matters, Sue's history included sexually promiscuous behavior from an early age. By the time she was sixteen, she had gotten pregnant and had an abortion. Sue's sexual past was such a deep source of shame that she had never revealed it to anyone, not even her husband. As the years passed, one of the ways she learned to control her pain was through avoidance. She was a master at redirecting conversations whenever they stirred up any unresolved pain from her past. Controlling conversations allowed her to cover her shame by hiding the emotions she kept locked inside.

She began to recognize that the consequences of sin were affecting her marriage—especially the areas of intimacy and sexuality. Sue was punishing herself. Deep down she didn't think she deserved to enjoy sex with her husband. So many times she wanted to talk to him about it, but she was gripped with fear. A record played over and over in her mind: *What if he can't forgive me? What if he judges me? What if my vulnerability only leads to more shame?* Her questions only escalated her fear, which led to more feelings of shame about her past. Once again, she tried to control her fear and hide her shame by withdrawing from her husband, blaming herself, and isolating emotionally (what we call the shame-blame-fear-control cycle).

I explained to Sue how this cycle works and challenged her to consider the many ways it was causing division in her marriage. Sue was perceptive and teachable. She immediately began to see some of the consequences of the Enemy's lies and of her own decision to protect herself. Over time she began to make some connections between her sexual promiscuity and issues related to her family of origin, specifically regarding her relationship with her father. The shame, blame, fear, and control she experienced as a young girl continued to play out in her marriage. She controlled through denial, manipulation, lying, and sexual rebellion. From a spiritual perspective, Sue knew that God forgave her, but she had never truly forgiven herself.

Sue opened her heart to God and asked Him for healing. For the first time, she forgave herself and was willing to receive God's forgiveness.

As we continued to meet, she addressed many of her fears and began to explore her control issues. God was beginning to reveal the lies that Sue had believed for so long, replacing them with His truth. She began to see herself as God saw her.

Understanding how the Enemy used the shame-blame-fear-control cycle in her life freed her to process her sexual history. Eventually she invited her husband to join her in counseling. Together they began to learn about God's original marriage design, and they started working through many difficult and painful issues—replacing shame, blame, fear, and control with intimacy, unity, and co-leading together, letting *unity trump disunity*.

It was exciting to watch Sue and her husband advance in their marriage relationship, but her experience reinforces the truth that many challenges in marriages can be traced back to the fall.

As we saw in the creation story, God's primary purpose for marriage is for a man and a woman who are both made in the image of God to **reflect** and **reveal** the plurality, character, and goodness of God through their relationship with Him, with each other, and with all whose lives they touch. We also saw that God appointed man and woman to *co-lead together* and **rule**, taking dominion over the earth. He declared this dominion mandate first in Genesis 1:26, then reaffirmed it directly to the man and woman in verse 28: "God blessed *them*; and God said to *them*, 'Be fruitful and multiply, and fill the earth, and subdue it; and *rule* over the fish of the sea and over the birds of the sky, and over every living thing that moves on the earth.'"

Remember, in the beginning God instituted the following authority structure:

> God
> Man and woman (co-leadership)
> Nature

In Eden the man and woman were mutually dependent on God and each other within their community of oneness. God assigned the authority to **rule** over the earth to both the man and the woman. As we noted before, He did not designate any hierarchy, headship, male leadership, or female subordination within the first marriage. The couple enjoyed mutual equality and mutual authority. Their identity was established through their relationship with God and affirmed by each other. They were naked and not ashamed. Pure, innocent, and without sin, *together* they celebrated the one-flesh relationship that is exclusive to marriage.

But the man and woman were not alone.

A SNAKE IN THE GARDEN

You may think you know this story, but our hope is that you'll give it another read-through; there may be something here that you've forgotten or missed or that you possibly might see for the first time.

Satan had entered the garden in the form of a serpent—and as a question mark to all God had told Adam and Eve. Keep that in mind. We don't have a lot of information about Satan, but the Bible describes a point in time before creation when Satan and a third of heaven's angels rebelled against divine authority and became fierce enemies of God. Since that time, Satan's mission has been straightforward: to steal, kill, and destroy.[1]

The Enemy must have been present during creation and watched the story unfold. And Satan must have heard God give man this command: "From any tree of the garden you may eat freely; but from the tree of the knowledge of good and evil you shall not eat, for in the day that you eat from it you will surely die."[2]

The tree was God's reminder that "I am God; you are not!" Satan knew that if he could get humans to eat from this one tree, he could take over rulership. Perhaps remembering his own frustration at being denied the role of God, Satan tried to get humans to disobey God by twisting His words.

He strategically approached the woman rather than the man. Maybe he knew that the woman was at a disadvantage since when God gave man the command to not eat from the Tree of Knowledge of Good and Evil, she had not yet been created out of man. She had not had the benefit of receiving the prohibition directly from God, although most people presuppose she heard about it from her husband.

Knowing this, the Enemy asked the woman, "Indeed, has God said, 'You shall not eat from any tree of the garden'?"[3] There's the question mark—remember?

Here's how it played out from there. First, Satan deliberately minimized the seriousness of God's command by misquoting one word. Satan suggested to the woman that God had *said*, but the text tells us that God had *commanded*.

Second, he purposefully misquoted God's command, asking, "Has God said, 'You shall not eat from any tree of the garden'?" But God's command clearly stated, "From any tree of the garden you may eat freely"—except from the Tree of Knowledge of Good and Evil.

The woman responded to the Enemy's lies by repeating what she had probably heard from the man: "From the fruit of the trees of the garden we may eat."[4] This is correct—God had said they could eat freely. She continued, "But from the fruit of the tree which is in the middle of the garden, God has said, 'You shall not eat from it or touch it, or you will die.'"[5] This is incorrect—God did not say, He commanded. The woman had picked up Satan's wording. Not only that, she added to God's command; He never said anything about touching the tree.

Seizing his opportunity, the serpent told the woman another lie: "You surely will not die! For God knows that in the day you eat from it your eyes will be opened, and you will be like God, knowing good and evil."[6]

The Enemy introduced suspicion by questioning God's goodness. He suggested that God was holding out on the woman. As is observed in a quote often attributed to Oswald Chambers, "The root of all sin is the suspicion that God is not good."

The woman's response to the serpent's lies and the woman and man's response to God after they sinned may be the most tragic scenes in the entire Bible. Eve rebelled against God and His authority, stepping into the smaller story with self as the main character. The text reads, "When the woman saw that the tree was good for food, and that it was a delight to the eyes, and that the tree was desirable to make one wise, she took from its fruit and ate; and she gave also to her husband with her, and he ate."[7] Her husband being "with her" implies that the man was nearby and watched in silence as this encounter unfolded.

PARADISE LOST

Satan's statements often include both truth and lies. He said, "For God knows that in the day you eat from [the Tree of Knowledge of Good and Evil] your eyes will be opened, and you will be like God."[8] One lie in Satan's statement was that after they ate from the tree, the man and woman would become "like God." One truth was that after they sinned, the eyes of both of them were opened.

However, Satan's positive spin that "your eyes will be opened" resulted in the man and woman realizing "that they were naked."[9] With this new knowledge of good and evil, the first couple's purity and innocence were replaced with shame. The knowledge of good and evil that was reserved solely for God opened the door to judging. This was originally God's role, not humans'. Judging out of the knowledge of good and evil introduced the destructive cycle of shame, blame, fear, and control.

Another lie of Satan as he deceived the woman was, "You surely will not die!"[10] However, contrary to Satan's assurance, that first bite of forbidden fruit ushered in death and separation from God.

The result of that first question mark was the destruction of the first couple's intimacy with God. The woman's desire for God was replaced with a desire for her husband.[11] Sin distorted the man and woman's intimacy with each other. After sin, a new marriage view was spawned—what we refer to as male rulership. The husband would now "rule over" his wife.[12]

THE SHAME-BLAME-FEAR-CONTROL CYCLE

After Adam and Eve sinned, God called out, "Where are you?"[13] Adam's response revealed the devastation already inflicted by sin: "I heard the sound of You in the garden, and I was afraid because I was naked; so I hid myself."[14] Sin opened the door to shame, blame, fear, and a desperate desire for control. *What if our nakedness is exposed? What if our actions are found out? Our only hope is to control the situation by hiding.* This would be the first of the countless hide-and-seek games men and women have played with God and with each other throughout history.

WHO TOLD YOU THAT YOU WERE NAKED?

We love God's response; it's one of our favorite passages in the entire Bible. God asked, "Who told you that you were naked?"[15] God is omniscient—He knows everything—so *why did God ask this question when He already knew the answer?* We believe God wanted to remind His children that shame does not come from Him.[16]

We often use the words *shame* and *guilt* interchangeably, but they really are two different things. Guilt is connected to a person's behavior. A person may experience feelings of guilt when they do something wrong. Shame, however, runs much deeper. It is the awful sense of "feeling uniquely and hopelessly flawed."[17] Shame convinces people that they are a mistake, bad, even defective.

> Shame sucks the very life out of a person as it causes him (or her) to live continually on guard, always afraid that someone is about to discover and expose their "flaw." The lie is that, "I am different." Of course, this is being "different" in a bad way.[18]

Sin is at the root of shame. Shame opens the door for fear. Fear says, *What if I'm found out? What if people reject me?* Fear opens the door to blame and control. Control says*, I will handle this. I will cover my sin* *(shame) so no one will discover the truth. I will control this situation by blaming others in an attempt to avoid pain and rejection.* People try to exert control in many active and passive ways, including through blame, withdrawal, emotional or physical separation, perfectionism, passive/aggressive behavior, criticism, judgment, pride, passivity, etc.

A person may use the shame-blame-fear-control cycle to self-protect in an attempt to avoid being exposed or rejected, but in reality this cycle entraps its victims, distorting the way people see themselves and how they relate to others. Specifically in marriage, the shame-blame-fear-control cycle can cause disunity and isolate a husband and wife from God and each other, much as it did when sin first entered the world.

The heart of God never shames His children. Why? Because every person is made in His image and can find his or her identity in Him. Therefore, God does not shame His children, even when they make mistakes. At times His voice is convicting, but it is never condemning. Are you ashamed of anything in your life? Does your shame cause fear? Do you ever wonder, *What if someone found out ...? If they only knew ...?* Do you ever try to control your shame by blaming others or by hiding from God, your spouse, or others?

THE DEVASTATING CONSEQUENCES OF SIN

As we return to the biblical story, we read God's response to the man's words of shame, blame, fear, and control; with the situation out in the open, God spelled out specific consequences to sin, all of which have a direct impact on marriage.

> And He said, "Who told you that you were naked? Have you eaten from the tree of which I commanded you not

to eat?" The man said, "The woman whom You gave to be with me, she gave me from the tree, and I ate." Then the LORD God said to the woman, "What is this you have done?" And the woman said, "The serpent deceived me, and I ate." [19]

It is interesting to note that neither the man nor the woman took responsibility for their disobedience. The man blamed his wife and then he blamed God; the woman blamed the serpent.[20]

For the Serpent ...

First, God cursed the serpent for his deception and declared enmity between the serpent and the woman. It's interesting that God specifically placed enmity—defined as "mutual hatred or ill will"—between the serpent and the woman. Makes us wonder: *why was enmity not placed between the serpent and the man?* Especially if—as some believe—man possesses a measure of intrinsic authority and a functional hierarchical leadership role. If that is true, wouldn't God have placed enmity between the man and the serpent—not between the woman and the serpent?

On the other hand, might God be telling us something about the discerning heart of a woman? Perhaps the woman's response to God—"The serpent deceived me, and I ate"—represents something significant. When confronted, the man blamed the woman and God, but the woman recognized the serpent as the deceiver. Might recognizing deception be an important component that reveals something about the feminine aspect in God's nature?

Nonetheless, after God cursed the serpent and before He addressed the man or woman, His Father's heart offered a glimmer of hope for humankind. God foreshadowed His redemptive plan by declaring that hope would come forth from the seed of a woman. Eve's descendants would bring forth the person of Jesus Christ. A Savior would come to earth, deal with Satan, take back dominion, and open the door for couples to reclaim God's original marriage design of mutual equality and mutual authority—*co-leading together.*

But in the meantime, more consequences were to come.

For the Woman ...

God said to the woman, "I will greatly multiply your pain in childbirth, in pain you will bring forth children; yet your desire will be for your husband, and he will rule over you."[21]

Originally, the woman was created to have her primary needs met through her relationship with God while celebrating mutual equality and mutual authority with her husband. When sin entered the world, God's original marriage plan of co-leadership was replaced with a new view of marriage: what we call male rulership. One result was that the woman's desire shifted from God to her husband.

We see this dynamic playing out in marriages today. A woman may look to her husband, rather than to God, to meet her needs for security and significance. This might be an indication that she is living under the consequences of the fall instead of living out God's original co-leadership marriage design.

Reviewing the woman's behavior makes us wonder, *Did she show a propensity toward independence when she responded to the serpent without including her husband, "who was with her"?* What if the woman was given a do-over? What if she resisted any propensity toward independence and exercised co-leadership by inviting her husband into the decision-making process? What if she had said, "Honey, I was not created when God told you which trees we could eat from; the serpent is telling me that it's okay to eat from this particular tree. Is that what God told you?"

Exercising dominion and co-leading together would have provided protection for the man, the woman, and their marriage. Unfortunately, the woman acted independently. She chose not to include God or her husband ... and the rest (as they say) is history.

How does this play out in real life? How do the consequences of the fall affect a wife's ability to co-lead together in unity and mutual authority with her husband? We frequently hear husbands express concern over what they see as their wife's misplaced priorities. For example, a man may feel like the children take precedence over their marriage. In her own defense, the wife may justify her relationship with the children by accusing her husband of being passive, being disinterested, or failing to engage. She may argue, "What do you expect me to do? I feel like a single parent most of the time. Besides, you are never here for me or the kids anyway!"

This form of processing leads to disunity and only contributes to what husbands describe as their wife's tendency to "fly solo." This scenario plays out in many ways. A wife may intentionally withhold information from her husband in regard to the children, relationships, purchases, or finances. She may control the situation by deciding what her husband needs to know and what he doesn't need to know. The wife may justify her independence by convincing herself that in excluding her husband she is "only trying to keep the peace and avoid marital chaos."

This form of independence is self-protective and is often a subtle attempt to control. Perhaps the wife feels rejected by her husband's passivity or control. Instead of processing her pain with him or seeking counsel from a third party, she takes control by leaving him out of her decision-making process. In an attempt to avoid conflict, her response fosters an illegitimate form of independence. A wife living independently may seem admirable at first glance. However, this behavior can cause disunity. In marriage, interdependence should always trump independence.

Life Is Lived in a Story

Recently, a woman approached us at a Marriage Advance and tearfully admitted, "I stopped including my husband years ago. Eventually, I guess I just fired him. His passivity and failure to engage has been such a source of pain for me. I thought if I acted independently, if I learned to depend on myself and not need him, I could avoid the pain." Breaking down, she continued, "But it doesn't work. The more independent I become, the more alone I feel."

This wife realized she had been deceived. Just like Eve, she believed that independence was better than interdependence. But this style of relating directly opposes the co-leadership that God intended for a husband and wife. It led this wife to step into the smaller story, where she became the main character and marriage was all about her. Do you see how these tendencies toward independence can be traced back to the fall?

For the Man...

God set forth the consequences for the man's disobedience:

> Because you have listened to the voice of your wife, and have eaten from the tree about which I commanded you, saying, "You shall not eat from it";

> *Cursed is the ground because of you;*
> *In toil you will eat of it*
> *All the days of your life.*
> *Both thorns and thistles it shall grow for you;*
> *And you will eat the plants of the field;*
> *By the sweat of your face*
> *You will eat bread,*
> *Till you return to the ground,*
> *Because from it you were taken;*
> *For you are dust,*
> *And to dust you shall return.*[22]

Just like the woman, in God's original marriage design, the man was created to have his primary needs for security and significance met through his relationship with God while celebrating mutual equality, mutual authority, and co-leadership with his wife. When the first couple sinned, the mutual authority of God's original marriage design was replaced with male rulership and forced female subordination.

Another consequence of the fall was that the man would suffer pain as he tried to make a living (from the ground), just as the woman would suffer pain in bearing children—"The ground once ruled by man now ruled him and eventually absorbed his being. His domain became his cemetery; his throne became his grave."[23] If we review the hierarchy established after sin, it is interesting to note that the man became subject to the ground (his work), which was where he came from. The woman became subject to the man, which was where she came from.

We see men living out the consequences of the fall today as their wives accuse them of giving their careers precedence over marriage and family. In self-defense, the man may justify his focus on work by blaming his wife—"Someone has to pay the bills. You complain that I work too much, but it sure didn't seem to be a problem when we bought the larger home or purchased the new car you thought we had to have. Which way do you want it? You'd better decide, because I'd love to work fewer hours!"

Does that retort remind you of Adam's defensive response when God questioned him about events in the garden? First the man blamed his wife, then God, and then he again blamed his wife: "The *woman* whom *You* gave to be with me, *she* gave me from the tree, and I ate."[24] He responded as a victim. Unfortunately, leading, standing up for his wife, taking personal responsibility, or engaging with the Enemy was not the man's first response.

If, as traditional-hierarchical-complementarian marriage proponents believe, man was created as the leader, the person to whom God gave the prohibitions and job of tending the garden, the person who had some God-given measure of authority ... *he certainly failed to step into any of these responsibilities.* Tragically the man chose the smaller story where he was the main character. It was all about him as his less-than-stellar response led to blaming God and shaming his bride.

Today we still see men playing the shame, blame, fear, and control game. Their shame opens the door to fear, so they control by blaming. This response communicates, "Life is all about me." Men try to cover their shame by blaming their spouse, kids, boss, in-laws, friends, neighbors, life circumstances, and even God. Reviewing the man's behavior, we wonder: *could a man's propensity toward blaming be traced back to the fall?*

In addition to blaming, another behavior we see in the man before the fall is his failure to engage. Again we wonder: *could the man have had a propensity toward passivity?* The text reads that after the woman ate the fruit, "she gave also to her husband with her, and he ate."[25] The serpent was trying to deceive Adam's wife, and Adam failed to engage—he remained passive. Adam knew God's command to not eat from the Tree of Knowledge of Good and Evil. But he did nothing. He failed to engage with the serpent or with his wife.

Today we still see husbands choosing passivity as a form of self-protection. This style of relating goes against the co-leadership God intended in His original marriage design.

What if Adam was given a do-over? What if he engaged in battle with the serpent and rescued his bride by declaring, "God commanded us to not eat from that tree. Do not believe the serpent. He is lying and trying to deceive. Serpent, in the authority God has given us ... we command you to leave us alone"?

But unfortunately Adam did not engage with the serpent or his wife.

CO-LEADERSHIP REPLACED WITH MALE RULERSHIP

The Enemy still works 24-7 to destroy marriages. Unfortunately many couples have abandoned God's original co-leadership marriage principles. They have settled for a counterfeit form of oneness that includes hierarchy and female subordination, both of which are direct results of the fall. Couples share the same last name, parent their children, serve at church, enjoy friends, and even share a bed. But too often they are selfish and self-focused. They've set aside the supernatural power, protection, and incredible possibilities available when they co-lead together—where *unity trumps disunity* and *marriage is not about me.*

Sin changed God's original marriage design.

God's original marriage design	Later marriage views
God	God
Man and woman (co-leadership)	Nature
Nature	Man
	Woman

Through lies and deceit the Enemy had achieved victory on the level of a cosmic Super Bowl. He stole the dominion and co-leadership that God had given to the man and woman and to future generations. After sin entered the story, different marriage views were spawned:

- Male rulership (Genesis 3:16)
- Traditional-hierarchical-complementarian
- Egalitarian

None of these marriage views that surfaced after sin were what God originally designed for man and woman. But is it really possible for couples to return to Eden and to co-leadership?[26]

CHAPTER 5

CO-LEADERSHIP REGAINED

CAN CO-LEADERSHIP BE REGAINED?

We understand that some people find it difficult to grab hold of the concept of mutual equality and mutual authority because they formulate their marriage theology *after* sin entered the story and co-leadership was replaced with male rulership. Others will endlessly debate their perceived "infallible" interpretations of a handful of controversial New Testament marriage passages related to headship, submission, and authority.

Nevertheless, everyone agrees that once sin entered the marriage story, the husband and wife's relationship with God and their togetherness and unity with each other were fractured and fragmented. Through his deception, the Enemy seized dominion in marriage and in other areas of life for thousands of years. But God is always in control. His very essence is love and goodness. His nature is such that He refuses to abandon us even when we sin and rebel. From the moment the man and woman sinned, God had a plan to provide humankind with a way to return to His original marriage design of co-leadership in mutual equality and mutual authority.

God's plan involved a Savior, Jesus Christ, coming forth from the life-giving seed of a woman to become the Way, the Truth, and the Life. In agreement with God the Father, the second Person of the Trinity came to earth to make the necessary payment for the sins of humankind. Jesus came to save the lost,[1] to destroy the works of the Enemy,[2] to reclaim that which was lost,[3] and to free the oppressed.[4]

When Jesus came to earth, women were without question among the most oppressed people. In Jesus's time, His treatment of women was revolutionary. In her book *Half the Church*, Carolyn Custis James wrote about Jesus's relationships with women:

> Women on Jesus' A-list of potential friends and recruits included prostitutes, adulteresses, a shunned Samaritan, insignificant widows, a ceremonially unclean woman, a dead twelve-year-old girl, and demon-possessed woman. Jesus regarded them with unheard-of respect and gave them his undivided attention, even (and perhaps deliberately) when men were around. He engaged women publicly in deep theological conversation in a culture where respectable men avoided public conversations with women. He entered their grief by weeping openly with them. He included women among his disciples, welcomed their friendship, forged strong bonds with them, was blessed and fortified by their spiritual ministries, and recruited them as leaders and kingdom builders.[5]

Life Is Lived in a Story

Let's revisit Jesus's story.

Taking on human form, Jesus was miraculously conceived and born to a pure young girl named Mary. Growing up, He advanced in stature and favor with God and man. Then at thirty years of age He was baptized in the Jordan River.

At this inauguration of Jesus's earthly ministry, we find God the Son, God the Holy Spirit, and God the Father all together just as when they first set the world spinning. When the Son walked into the water to be baptized, the Holy Spirit made His appearance in the form of a dove and descended upon Jesus. At the same time God the Father declared His presence and confirmed His love for the Son: "This is My beloved Son, in whom I am well-pleased."[6] It's important to note that this declaration came *before* Jesus began His earthly ministry, which means the Father was pleased with the Son *before* He did anything.

The assurance of the Father's pleasure even before Jesus did anything must have given the Son encouragement for the difficult time He was about to face. Following Jesus's baptism, the Holy Spirit led Him into the desert for a divine appointment with Satan. Jesus spent forty days praying and fasting in preparation for this power encounter between good and evil.

Then the battle began.

IF YOU ARE ...

The Enemy fired his first missile: "If you are the Son of God, tell these stones to become bread."[7] The Devil launched a direct attack on Jesus's identity with this challenge: "If you are the Son of God..." Jesus responded by quoting Scripture: "It is written: 'Man shall not live on bread alone, but on every word that comes from the mouth of God.'"[8] Jesus knew who He was. In the strength of His identity, He stood on the Word of God.

The second attack was also aimed at Jesus's identity. The Devil took Him into Jerusalem and had Him stand on the pinnacle of the temple:

> "If you are the Son of God," he said, "throw yourself down. For it is written:
>
> *'He will command his angels concerning you,*
> *and they will lift you up in their hands,*
> *so that you will not strike your foot against a stone.'"[9]*

Again Jesus responded by quoting Scripture: "It is also written: 'Do not put the Lord your God to the test.'"[10]

The Enemy is not very creative. He still uses the same strategy, trying to get us to question our true identity, our connection with God. He knows the insidious danger that comes when we focus on ourselves, whether we are standing on a mountaintop where everything is going great or wandering alone in the desert.

Jesus understood the truth all of us need to remember: *it's not about me.* Every aspect of life, including marriage, is about God. He invites every spouse to live in the Larger Story, where God is the main character. Most people tend to live in the smaller story, where self takes center stage as the main character. And selfishness lies at the core of every sin.

> In every sin we can see self at work. Although people today classify sins into an untold number of categories, yet inductively speaking there is but one basic sin: all the

thoughts and deeds which are sins are related to "self."
... All sins are committed for the sake of the self. If the
element of self is missing, there will be no sin.... Wherever
sin is, there is the activity of the self.[11]

Jesus chose not to make self the main character in His story, even in the face of the Devil's determined attacks. For his third attempt, Satan took Jesus to a very high mountain and showed Him all the kingdoms of the world and their splendor. He said, "All this I will give you ... if you will bow down and worship me."[12] How did Jesus respond? Yet again He quoted Scripture and pointed out that the story is about God, not self: "Away from me, Satan! For it is written: 'Worship the Lord your God, and serve him only.'"[13] What was the result? "When the devil had finished every temptation, he left Him until an opportune time."[14]

It is significant to note that Jesus never questioned the Devil's claim that he could deliver all the kingdoms of the world. Why? Because He knew Satan had stolen dominion from Adam and Eve in the garden. In Eden the woman faced three temptations and was offered three promises. The Enemy told her that if she ate the fruit her eyes would be opened, she would be like God, and she would know good and evil. The woman made herself the point of reference—it was all about her. In Eden Satan stole the dominion meant for man and woman. Therefore, he had authority to offer Jesus the kingdoms; otherwise, it would not have been a true temptation. Thankfully, Jesus took on human form and came to earth to restore *that* which was lost.[15] "That" which was lost included the dominion and mutual authority God gave to its rightful owners—both men and women.

Although Satan was mortally wounded in these New Testament power encounters, he has not given up the fight. The battle between good and evil continues. The Enemy continues to question the goodness of

God, and he continues to lie and distort God's truths. Just as he did to Jesus, the Enemy questions a person's identity—their position as a son or daughter made in the image of a good Father. He tries to convince us that he still has dominion and authority. Thankfully, Jesus Christ defeated Satan. Among countless other good things, this means we can figuratively return to Eden and God's original togetherness in co-leadership design for marriage.

THE STRENGTH AND PROTECTION OF COVENANT

In order for a Christian couple to fulfill God's purpose to co-lead in marriage, they must be in covenant. A covenant is far more binding than a contract or commitment. In the Bible, a covenant with God involved death: "For where a covenant is, there must of necessity be the death of the one who made it."[16] A biblical marriage covenant includes three parties: God, one man, and one woman. Therefore, a marriage covenant involves the husband and wife each dying to themselves as they choose to live for God and their spouse.

This idea of death can sound scary unless you recognize that covenant between a husband, a wife, and God provides power and protection. The book of Ecclesiastes says, "Though one may be overpowered, two can defend themselves. A cord of three strands is not quickly broken."[17] Like a cord with three strands, covenant provides strength in marriage because each partner is in relationship with God and each other. This enables them to give themselves fully to the purposes of God, to their spouse, and to others. Through living out covenant and co-leading together, a husband and wife are able to **reflect** and **reveal** the plurality and goodness of God.

Walking out covenant within God's original marriage design involves an ongoing process of dying to selfishness and growing in intimacy with

God and each other. The power, protection, and authority a couple has within the exclusivity of the marriage covenant provide unlimited life-giving potential for the husband and the wife to powerfully impact each other, others, and the kingdom of God

In addition to exclusivity, a marriage covenant includes permanence. A husband and wife commit to walking together for their entire lives. A lifetime is a long time, and every marriage will experience obstacles— "those who marry will face many troubles."[18] Entering into a marriage covenant involves a husband and wife promising God and each other that they will stay together no matter what: "for better or for worse, for richer or for poorer, in sickness and in health, to love, honor, and cherish, until death do us part." Throughout thirty-eight years of marriage, we've raised children, switched careers, moved a number of times, and become grandparents. But the constant through every life experience has been walking out covenant and co-leading together.

God designed marriage for a husband and wife to do life together in cov-enant as "one." They are to leave other significant relationships, cleave to each other, and become one flesh. Becoming one flesh highlights sexual intercourse in marriage. God uniquely created a husband and wife so they can merge together physically—become one flesh—and **reproduce** human beings made in God's image and representing both the masculine and feminine characteristics of God. Becoming one flesh also includes advancing in spirit and soul oneness—in intimacy—knowing and being fully known.

WALKING COVENANT OUT DAY BY DAY

Walking out spirit-soul-body oneness is an ongoing process of growing in intimacy with God and each other. In our marriage, a key to advancing in oneness is understanding how God has individually wired and gifted us. Even after decades of marriage, we are still learning, but we have studied ourselves and each other to help discern our passions, temperaments, love languages, and spiritual gifts.

We believe marriage is an invitation for couples to step into the unique blessings and benefits of "two becoming one." In all sincerity, our experience suggests that God's original co-leadership marriage design is much more difficult to live out than other marriage views we have observed. This is because waiting on God for agreement and unity exposes selfishness, control, rebellion, and manipulation.

Frankly, often our marriage would be easier if Tim just took charge. With his personality, temperament, and leadership gifts, he could easily step into traditional marriage views, where the husband functions as the leader who has responsibility and the final say in the decision-making process.

However, throughout our marriage, we have determined that our marriage works best when we walk out co-leadership and obey the biblical commands to "be subject to one another in the fear of Christ"[19] and "with humility of mind regard one another as more important than yourselves."[20] In regard to authority, we focus on *mutual authority.* In the apostle Paul's letter to the church in Corinth, he wrote, "The wife does not have *authority* over her own body, but the husband does; and likewise also the husband does not have *authority* over his own body, but the wife does."[21] This text clearly commands *mutual authority* to both the husband and wife.

In our marriage we reach decisions as we individually **I.O.T.L.** *(inquire of the Lord)* and then wait for unity. We do not walk out our marriage covenant or make final decisions based on gender. In what we refer to as the male rulership marriage view or the traditional-hierarchical-complementarian marriage view, gender trumps all else in the decision-making process. The husband assumes the role as the leader who has functional authority over his wife. Our experience is that in each of these marriage views, the benefits of co-leading together in mutual authority are compromised.

Life Is Lived in a Story

anne

A recent experience in our marriage provides a great illustration of how we live in covenant and co-lead in unity. The two of us have worked together in marriage ministry for over twenty-five years. All along we thought that leading our own marriage ministry full-time was a strong probability ... someday.

Fifteen years ago we took a leap of faith when Tim resigned from his twenty-plus-year fire department career. We left the Chicago suburbs—saying good-bye to family, friends, a great church, the security and benefits of a successful career, and a lifetime of relationships—in response to God's invitation to serve at a church in Holland, Michigan. After five years there, God invited us to move our family to California. This involved selling almost everything we owned so we could move into an apartment in Pasadena. From California, God invited us to move to Colorado Springs, where we currently live.

Then over seven years ago, Tim felt God was calling us to begin REAL LIFE Ministries full-time.

On the wall of his office hangs a quote: "Leap and the net will appear!" Tim is a natural-born risk taker whose deep trust frees him to joyfully follow wherever God leads. He was ready to take the plunge.

On the other hand, I am not a risk taker. I prefer to see the net appear *before* I leap. I'm not sure whether this is a lack of faith or a sign of stability. In any case, leaving our full-time jobs to begin our own ministry—giving up the security of two salaries and the benefits of an insurance and retirement plan—felt to me less like a step of faith and more like free-falling off a cliff. Although I shared Tim's dream of ministering to marriages full-time, I struggled with fear. Many nights I lay awake wondering, *Is this faith or foolishness? What if our ministry doesn't flourish and we lose everything? What if we get in over our heads and the work consumes us? What if ...?*

Tim was ready to move forward, convinced the timing was God's. But over the years we've agreed never to make decisions until we both **I.O.T.L.** and are in agreement about what we sense Him saying—because, as we've talked about before, our marriage motto is *unity trumps disunity*. Waiting until we are in agreement is one practical way we live out covenant and our commitment to co-lead together, and we believe this provides our marriage with power and protection.

So Tim agreed to wait on me, and we continued to process together. While we were not in agreement on when to leave our jobs, we did agree on a number of other things. We agreed we definitely needed to downsize in order to adjust to not having a six-figure income as well as regular paychecks. As a first step, we agreed to put our house up for sale. In October we found a smaller home and took another step of faith by putting money down on it. It seemed as if God was opening one door at a time as we walked in agreement with Him and each other. We were scheduled to close on the house in the spring, giving us plenty of time to sell our home. But months passed without a single offer. In March we became owners of two homes and two mortgage payments. This made it impossible for us to quit our jobs and go into full-time marriage ministry. Our frustration and stress levels were high, but Tim still believed this was God's timing. My fears and what-if questions continued as we waited for the house to sell. We committed to pray and fast and wait on God.

One night I awoke from a deep sleep in which I had a vivid dream that I knew was from God. It wasn't the kind of dream with a story line but one that spoke directly to my heart. I heard two words in my dream: *wiggle room*. When I woke up I knew exactly what those two words meant. Wiggle room refers to having just enough space to "wiggle out" of something. It's like having a safety net or an emergency escape exit ... just in case. For a person who is not a risk taker, having wiggle room is very important.

The next morning as Tim and I drove together to work, I told him about my dream and what I thought it meant: "The words *wiggle room* represent my fears. Fear and indecision provide a safety net for me so I won't have to step out in faith. When I woke up last night I realized that indecision is a subtle form of control. I think God wants me to address my fears instead of letting them control me. I need to focus on God and His power instead of focusing on fear."

When we got to work, Tim stopped the car. I looked over at him and said, "I'm finally ready for both of us to quit our jobs and begin REAL LIFE Ministries full-time. God has been preparing us for this next step of faith. It's time. If you're still up for it, I'm ready to take this leap of faith with you—*together*."

Knowing we were both in agreement provided us with the strength and protection we needed to move forward in unity. Together we prayed, *Lord, You know we are carrying two house payments. We have lowered our price three times and have not gotten one offer. How can we leave our jobs and lose our salaries and benefits? Should we put both houses up for sale? Is this Your timing for us? We are trusting that this leading is from You and that You will provide a way.*

In our decision-making process, Tim and I include not only God and each other but also a trusted group of friends. When we both decided to quit our jobs, Tim and I joined friends and family in praying together. We found it encouraging that, after praying, every person we included affirmed our direction, saying, "As crazy as it sounds, I think you are supposed to take this leap of faith."

One night neither of us slept a wink. We tossed and turned, seeking God's direction. In the morning Tim said he sensed our resignation date should be effective June 5. That was only two months away. Tim made it crystal clear that we would only do this if we both had "green lights" and felt certain it was God's desire—with no wiggle room. I again faced my fears about giving up our financial security net. I poured my heart out to the Lord and sensed His confirmation. The next day we met with our bosses, explained our process, and handed in our letters of resignation.

On June 5 we drove home from our last day at work—no jobs, no income, no benefits, and two mortgage payments. My wiggle room was like an old friend who had left town. The very next day, after over six months without one single offer on our home, our realtor called to schedule an appointment for a couple to look at the house. They were preapproved and had nothing to sell. A few days later this couple made an offer on our house.

They made only one stipulation: they needed to move in immediately. God was affirming our adventure.

Looking back now, we see that God was teaching us about the power in agreement and the protection that comes through covenant and co-leading in unity. Over the years, waiting for marital unity has saved us from making countless unwise decisions.

AN EXPERIMENT IN UNITY

We believe most couples want to advance in marriage. However, we've seen that more often, people focus on what their husband or wife needs to change—rather than inviting God and their spouse to identify and help make changes in *them*. God created every person with the freedom to choose. You are free to choose whom you will serve, whom you will follow, and whose authority you will submit to. You can choose to submit to and follow God, the Enemy, others, or yourself.

In a similar way, every married couple has a choice as to how they walk out marriage. Because Jesus took back dominion from Satan, husbands and wives are free to return to the co-leadership God originally intended for them. The life-giving message of the New Testament reminds every couple that "sin shall not have dominion over you, for you are not under law but under grace."[22]

With this in mind we encourage couples to figuratively return to Eden and prayerfully revisit God's original *togetherness* in co-leadership marriage design. Your choice to honor covenant and live together in mutual authority and mutual equality will advance God's kingdom and impact not only your marriage but also your children, your spiritual children, and future generations.

CHAPTER 6

DID JESUS SAY ANYTHING ABOUT MARRIAGE?

Life Is Lived in a Story

tim

At a REAL LIFE Marriage Advance, a woman we will refer to as Rachel approached us and said, "Your co-leadership—*unity trumps disunity*—teaching is stirring something in my heart. Can I ask about Jesus? Did He teach anything about marriage?"

We answered, "That's a great question—what *was* Jesus's view on marriage? Some Pharisees wanted to know the same thing. They came to test Jesus with questions about marriage and divorce. It's important to remember that Jesus came to earth during a season of history where women were treated as property. Patriarchy, misogyny, hierarchy, and forced female subordination led to extreme abuses. In marriages, the male rulership view prevailed in both religious and pagan cultures."

Rachel asked, "Can you give me an example of how women were treated as property in that season of history?"

"We'll try. Let's look at the story in Genesis 19 about two angels coming to Sodom. Lot met them and insisted they come to his home to spend the night. In the evening the men of the city surrounded the house and demanded Lot give the visitors to them to have homosexual relations with. Do you recall how Lot responded?"

"I recall the story you are referring to," Rachel told us, "but I don't remember what Lot said."

We told her the story. "Lot went out to the angry mob, shut the door behind him, and said, 'Please, my brothers, do not act wickedly. Now behold, I have two daughters who have not had relations with man; please let me bring them out to you, and do to them whatever you like; only do nothing to these men, inasmuch as they have come under the shelter of my roof—'"[1]

Rachel interrupted. "How could Lot offer his two virgin daughters to be abused—possibly killed—by a mob of angry men in order to protect two strangers when he had only known them for a few hours?"

"Because the demands of hospitality—of a host to protect his guests at all costs—trumped the safety and purity of his two daughters. This is just one example of the shameful treatment and abuses of women. Hopefully it gives you a glimpse into the historical and cultural context of the marriage and divorce question Jesus was being asked by the Pharisees."

Rachel replied, "But that example is from thousands of years ago. It's not like we can historically verify that account. Can you give me a more current example?"

"I will try," I told her. "Our youngest daughter, Cate, is a social worker. After graduating with her master's degree from Jane Addams College in Chicago, she was selected for a yearlong fellowship at Children's Hospital in Boston, where she worked with the pediatric palliative care team. I visited her, and she took me to Plymouth, Massachusetts, and the site of the Mayflower landing. On a hill overlooking the water is a burial crypt that contains the remains of the women and men who risked their lives coming to America—many of whom died on the trip overseas.

"As I stood in front of this monument and read the names, it dawned on me that the names engraved to honor these brave founders of our country were only men's names. Remember this was a season of history where women were treated as second-class citizens in church and society. A Christian husband—as *head* was defined at the time—ruled over his wife. The husband was the person in charge, the one who had absolute authority. As each woman and man who helped found our country died, their remains were placed in this crypt; however, on this memorial plaque, only male names are recognized.

"But thankfully, God still speaks, and over time views about authority and headship have dramatically changed. For example, can you imagine the Vietnam or 9/11 memorials listing only men's names and excluding women's?"

Rachel said, "That would be tragic and discriminatory. But help me understand, how does all this relate to Jesus's view of marriage?"

"Rachel, the culture Jesus was born into followed centuries of misogyny, which is defined as 'a hatred of women as a sexually defined group'[2] and patriarchy, which is defined as 'a social system in which men are regarded as the authority within the family and society, and in which power and possessions are passed on from father to son.'[3] The culture was also full of countless abuses of women. Yet when Jesus was questioned about divorce and remarriage, where did He go for His marriage model? Similar to the apostle Paul in the Ephesians chapter that introduces headship, Jesus went back to the beginning, to Genesis, before sin entered the picture. He did not cite the male rulership marriage view—'your desire will be for your husband, and he will rule over you.'[4] Nor did Jesus's words reflect the perspective of later New Testament writers who were addressing specific marriage issues in specific places at specific times in history. Jesus never mentioned headship, submission, or the husband being the leader or spiritual cover. Jesus did not give any preference toward the male rulership, traditional-hierarchical-complementarian, and egalitarian marriage views."

"Then exactly how did Jesus describe marriage?" Rachel asked.

THE PHARISEES TEST JESUS

"Here's the question the Pharisees asked, Rachel: 'Is it lawful for a man to divorce his wife for any and every reason?'[5]

"The Pharisees came to test Jesus's understanding of divorce. First off, in our opinion the Pharisees asked Jesus the wrong question. If they truly had a heart for God's design for marriage, a better question would have been: *Jesus, how can troubled marriages be saved?* Instead, as religious leaders who at that time had absolute authority over women, they asked Jesus to comment on reasons a husband could divorce his wife."

"We love how Jesus responded. He began with a rhetorical question: *Haven't you read* … Jesus knew the Pharisees were well versed in the Scriptures. As we envision this scene, we see Jesus responding to what the Pharisees think is a trick question about divorce. He redirects them to a key pre-fall marriage text—no doubt a passage they had read many times. And Jesus boldly quotes God's original marriage design:

> Haven't you read ... that at the beginning the Creator 'made them male and female,' and said, 'For this reason a man will leave his father and mother and be united to his wife, and the two will become one flesh'? So they are no longer two, but one flesh. Therefore what God has joined together, let no one separate.[6]

"Remember, Rachel—during that season of history the *woman* was the one required to leave her home, with a dowry, to be married and cleave to her husband as she obediently obeyed and served him the rest of her life. At that time a wife was treated like property, and a husband could divorce a wife for any reason by merely writing his decision to divorce on a piece of paper. We believe Jesus understood that the motive beneath the Pharisees' question was more about male superiority and forced female subordination. Notice how Jesus turned the table on these religious leaders and reminded them that in the beginning the *man* was commanded to leave his home and cleave to his wife. We suspect that the ways Jesus honored women as He quoted this passage and redirected the divorce question to God's original marriage design was a radical response to the Pharisees, certainly not what these religious leaders were expecting.

"It's also interesting to note another perspective in the Matthew 19 text that affirms how poorly women were treated during that season of history. Remember that the disciples (many of whom were married) were present during Jesus's encounter with the Pharisees. After Jesus's unheard-of gender statement to the Pharisees, the disciples responded to Jesus: 'If the relationship of the man and his wife is like [Jesus described God's original marriage design] it is better not to marry.'[7] Notice that there is no question mark at the end of their statement. The disciples do not ask, 'Is it better not to marry?' Instead they declare: 'It is better not to marry.' Our point is that even Jesus's disciples, the patriarchs of the faith, who were martyred during the early years of the church and authored much of the New Testament, were not in touch with God's original design for marriage. Similar to the Pharisees, Jesus's disciples were still under the strong influence of patriarchy, male rulership, and forced female subordination. That is why Jesus's treatment of women was so over-the-top countercultural."[8]

Rachel asked, "But if Jesus wanted to make a clear statement about equality, why did He select only males to be His disciples? Why didn't He select six males and six females?"

"That's a fair question, Rachel. One could suggest that since Jesus came to die for the sins of Jews and Gentiles, He should have selected six Jewish males and six Gentile males. Furthermore, if Jesus wanted to make a bold statement about Jews, Gentiles, males, and females, then why didn't He select six males—three Jews and three Gentiles—and six females—three Jews and three Gentiles?"

Rachel asked us, "But what are your thoughts about Jesus selecting twelve Jewish men?"

"Rachel, first consider a more recent historical example—the abolition of slavery. Abraham Lincoln was passionate about racial equality and eliminating slavery. But it would have been political suicide for him to choose an African-American to run as his vice president. The people in that season of history would have unilaterally rejected Lincoln and his equality message. Similarly, Jesus operated within the cultural and historical framework He was born into. Therefore, He wisely chose only male

Jewish disciples. This opened the door for Him to relate to the culture and promote His kingdom-of-God message. Stop for a moment and consider the fallout had He selected Gentiles or females as part of His group of twelve disciples: people would have unilaterally rejected Jesus and His message."

Rachel said, "I see your point. But here's another question I have. When I talk with my Christian friends, it seems like there is so much stress and drama over equality, headship, submission, and authority in marriage. Why don't more couples live out God's original co-leadership marriage principles?"

"That's a great question. We're not sure. Our sense is we are still dealing with centuries of patriarchal abuses, plus the religious spirit is alive and well—operating full-time (overtime) in many churches, denominations, and seminaries.[9] And always remember there is an Enemy in all this who understands the supernatural power, protection, and kingdom-advancing potential in God's original co-leadership marriage principles. Fortunately, the Enemy is not very creative; just as he attacked the first married couple—through lies, deception, and questioning God's goodness—the Enemy continues to use his limited power to do everything to mess with marriage.

"But you know, Rachel, after observing marriage for decades, our sincere sense is God is in the incipient stage of birthing a much-needed marriage reformation. Our prayer and heart's desire is that we can be early adopters in this miraculous movement of God."

As we wrapped up our conversation, we thanked Rachel and encouraged her to prayerfully review the passages we'd talked about, as well as her biblical method of interpretation. We explained to her that our experience is often a person takes a dogmatic, legalistic, hard-line, *if-the-plain-sense-makes-sense-seek-no-other-sense* approach; or cuts and pastes or absolutizes a certain text; or tries to build his or her position on things that are implied; or incorporates selective literalism to controversial texts as a basis for his or her theology. In our experience, when this happens, problems quickly surface.

God is all about relationship, and marriage **reflects** relationship. Remember, walking out relationship with God and a spouse is a lifelong journey. We agree with professor and author Scot McKnight, who said, "For far too many, conversion is seen as a Birth Certificate instead of a Driver's License.... Conversion is a marriage rather than the Marriage Certificate."[10] Just as marriage is a commitment to a lifetime of growing in intimacy with a spouse, so the person who makes a decision to repent of his or her sins and begin a relationship with Jesus enters into a lifelong journey of growing in intimacy and relationship with God.

THE WHY OF MARRIAGE—THE 4 R'S

As we conclude Part 1 we want to revisit an important question: *why* did God create marriage?

God created marriage to invite a man and woman to enter into covenant with God and each other, to *co-lead together* in mutual equality and mutual authority, and to:

> **Reflect and Reveal**: God's plurality and nature; mutual equality; *both* made in God's image
>
> **Rule**: co-lead *together*; mutual authority; *both* given the dominion (rulership) mandate
>
> **Reproduce**: be fruitful and multiply; *both* given the procreation mandate

We have explored **reflect**, **reveal**, and **rule**; let's finish Part 1 by reviewing the **reproduce** command to married couples.

"BE FRUITFUL AND MULTIPLY AND FILL THE EARTH ..."

Marriage and having children are intimately related. Beginning with the first married couple, God commands a husband and wife to **reproduce**— to "be fruitful and multiply."[11] All children have intrinsic value because they are made in the image of God. In marriage, having children (including adopting and having spiritual children) provides opportunities to **reproduce** and teach children life-giving godly values that are to be passed on to future generations. With children ages thirty-six, thirty-five, thirty-three, and twenty-eight—plus five grandchildren—we understand that parenting provides countless invitations to live out "it is not about me."

That said, we have found that the joys and challenges in parenting (and grandparenting) are without measure. Fyodor Dostoevsky touched on the power of being with children: "the soul is healed by being with children." However, it's important to note that in addition to the procreation mandate of being fruitful, multiplying, and filling the earth, we believe God created intimacy and sexuality for more than the purpose of procreation. We will briefly review five of God's purposes for marital intimacy and sexuality. This non-exhaustive list includes: celebration, procreation, protection, pleasure, and comfort.

1. Marital Sex Is for *Celebration.*

The first thing we learn about marriage from the creation story is that every man and every woman are made in the image of God.[12] Maleness and masculinity are an intrinsic part of every man. Femaleness and femininity are an intrinsic part of every woman. One man and one woman are intrinsic parts of every marriage. Therefore, God invites a married couple—individually and together—to celebrate their creational design.

Colossians 3:17 says, "Whatever you do in word or deed, do all in the name of the Lord Jesus." *All* includes sexual intimacy. Sex within the permanence and exclusivity of marriage can become an act of worship toward God, the Creator of sex. Marriage becomes an invitation for couples to love, serve, complement, and enjoy each other. In marriage a man and woman are invited to celebrate intimacy and sexuality as *together* they rejoice in being "naked and not ashamed."

2. Marital Sex Is for **Procreation.**

The sexual dimension in marriage is very powerful. Married couples are commanded to be fruitful and multiply. Keep in mind that being fruitful and multiplying is not limited to having biological children—it includes adoption, foster parenting, and spiritual parenting. Nevertheless, although fatherhood and motherhood are extremely important, always remember that a person's highest calling is to love God with all his or her heart, soul, mind, and strength.[13]

3. Marital Sex Is for **Protection.**

Sex creates a strong bond between a husband and wife, a bond that helps protect the marriage relationship. The Enemy clearly understands the power of sexuality and uses sexual temptation as one of his key strategies to destroy intimacy and marriages. A healthy sex life helps a couple avoid temptation.[14]

Couples who enjoy a healthy sexual relationship feel more connected and emotionally focused on each other as well as more hopeful about their marriage. Studies also indicate that a healthy sex life protects a couple from health problems. Positive endorphins and Oxytocin released during orgasm help suppress stress and aid the body in self-healing and overall better health.

4. Marital Sex Is for **Pleasure.**

Despite anything you may have heard to the contrary, God is pro-sex and pro-pleasure. His desire is for marital couples to enjoy a mutually satisfying sex life. God created orgasms so a couple could experience deep pleasure and physical satisfaction through sexual intimacy within their marriage. A husband and wife are invited by God to *eat, drink, and imbibe deeply*.[15]

5. Marital Sex Is for **Comfort.**

After the death of David and Bathsheba's son, the Bible says, "Then David comforted his wife Bathsheba, and went in to her and lay with her."[16] During difficult times in marriage, providing comfort through sexual expression can be a gift from God. Instead of viewing pain, loss, and crises as obstacles, spouses can use them as opportunities to step into the Larger Story and advance in intimacy. Strengthening marital bonds by serving a spouse sexually in difficult times can bring comfort and healing.

+ + +

The Bible is clear: God is pro-sex. He designed sex in marriage for celebration, procreation, protection, pleasure, and comfort. All of these purposes for sexual intimacy in marriage are to be walked out in purity: "Let marriage be held in honor among all, and let the marriage bed be undefiled."[17] Honor includes "personal integrity; respect; dignity"[18]; defiled means "to make something dirty or polluted."[19] Sexual intimacy in marriage is to be pure and undefiled. Our culture assaults men and women with impure and defiled pictures and portrayals of marriage and sexuality. Men and women must reject these assaults and advance in reclaiming the purity and sanctity of a husband and wife "becoming one," celebrating being "naked and not ashamed."

Unfortunately, the sexual dimension in many marriages is far from what God intended. Working with couples for decades, we've reached the conclusion that husbands and wives who focus the majority of their efforts solely on intercourse and orgasm miss out on all that God has intended for sexual intimacy in marriage. Important as orgasms are, a key to an exhilarating sex life involves passionately pursuing a spouse's heart, mind, soul, and body.

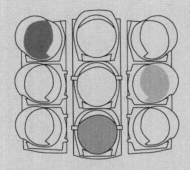

PART TWO

Putting Co-Leadership into Practice

There shall be such a oneness between you

that when one weeps,

the other shall taste salt.

Author Unknown

CHAPTER 7

FROM "ME" TO "WE"

THE MYSTERY OF MARRIAGE

When describing marriage, the apostle Paul used a unique word: *mystery*. A mystery is something difficult to fully understand or explain. Often a mystery is something that unfolds over time.

This makes us wonder—why did Paul use the word *mystery* to describe marriage? Could God's Trinitarian mystery be similar to the mystery in marriage Paul referred to?

The mystery in marriage involves two individuals—one man and one woman—both created in the image of God, both invited to **reflect** and **reveal** the plurality in the *mystery* of God's Trinitarian nature.

We resonate with Charles Spurgeon's take on being open to mysteries and things we do not yet know. He said, "I intend to grasp tightly with one hand the truths I have already learned, and to keep the other hand wide open to take in the things I do not yet know."[1]

Life Is Lived in a Story

anne

The two of us have experienced many miraculous moments together, but few things compare to the birth of our first child. Holding our son for the first time was one of those moments that will be locked in my heart forever. When the doctor placed him in my arms, Tim and I just stared at him for the longest time. We scanned every inch of his perfect little body. We were overwhelmed with the gift that God had entrusted to us. As we looked into the eyes of this new life, there was a moment when we actually felt as if the three of us were one.

During those first days, our hospital room was flooded with visitors, flowers, and cards. Everyone was celebrating Timmy's arrival. My family would hold him and say, "He looks just like your baby pictures." Tim's family held him and said, "He's definitely an Evans." Each family saw in our son something familiar—similarities inherited from both of us. Yet as we stared into his eyes we knew that he was much more than a reflection of his mom and dad. Although Timmy represents each of us in different ways, although his genes come directly from the two of us, he is miraculously much more than a simple equation of tim+anne = Timmy. God carefully crafted him as an entirely new creation, full of amazing wonders and life-giving potential.

Just as a baby is more than the sum of his parents' contributed parts, so a marriage can be much greater than just the two people involved—when God is included in the relationship.

THE BIRTH OF A MARITAL "WE"

Two becoming one in marriage is *not* about a loss of personal identity—it is a process where both partners' identities are enhanced. Marriage is about more than "you" plus "me." When a husband and wife become one, a spiritual transaction takes place. "You" and "me" becomes "we."

When two people enter into covenant with God and each other, a new life—a "we" life—is created. This one-of-a-kind husband-wife intimacy is critical to living out marriage as God designed. Marital oneness becomes the pathway for couples to figuratively return to the co-leadership marriage principles of Eden and together **reflect** and **reveal** God's plurality and nature.

The good news is every husband and wife can choose to co-lead *together*. This includes co-leading in their home, finances, emotions, and sexual relationship. Co-leadership includes raising children and passing on godly values to future generations. When a couple co-leads together, they exchange a "me" perspective for a "we" perspective. They celebrate the unity and diversity intrinsic in God's original design of mutual equality (both made in the image of God) and mutual authority (both given the procreation and dominion mandates).

Marriage is designed to be an exclusive and permanent relationship in which a husband and wife continually draw closer in intimacy with God and each other. Dr. Gilbert Bilezikian, our professor at Wheaton College, defined intimacy as "to know and be fully known."[2] As a person grows in knowing and being fully known by God and his or her spouse, that person grows in intimacy and relationship.

Marriage is a place where love is supposed to rule. Our experience is that love responds to love—and love always leaves a mark. Similarly, control responds to control. Couples can choose love over control. They can choose not to hide from God or each other, and they can risk removing emotional fig leaves as they **reflect** and **reveal** the goodness of God to each other. In marriage the key is for couples to focus on co-leadership. Practically, this involves implementing the **Traffic Light Principle**.

You'll remember we began in chapter 1 with the **Traffic Light Principle**. We said that principle alone could change your marriage if you gave it a try. We stand by that. But the story that follows raises a very important point about this principle—one that makes all the difference.

BEN'S QUESTION ("ME" MUST INCLUDE "THEE")

At a recent REAL LIFE Marriage Advance, a man we will refer to as Ben stood up and asked, "If your co-leadership slogan *unity trumps disunity* is true, can't couples have unity and still mess up? Because there have been times when my wife and I have been on the same page and we were in agreement. Yet the decision we made together ended up being a total disaster. My question is, can a husband and wife be in unity and be wrong?"

We thanked Ben for his question and explained to him, "We are not saying *agreement is it*. Let's go back to the first married couple in the garden of Eden. Adam and Eve were in agreement when they both choose to eat the forbidden fruit. Yet their agreement did not provide power and protection; in fact it ended in death and devastation." We asked him, "Ben, what are the steps in the **Traffic Light Principle**?"

He responded, "My wife and I try to co-lead together and make decisions when we both have a green light; if we have different lights we do not make the decision."

"That's correct."

"But," he said, "I can think of times when my wife and I both had green lights and it ended up being a disaster."

We explained to Ben, "You and your wife may be implementing only part of the **Traffic Light Principle**. Just having agreement as a couple does not in and of itself guarantee power and protection in the decision-making process. An example would be a couple agreeing to charge thousands of dollars on credit when they just lost their jobs. Even though they agreed, this would be an unwise decision. However, there is an important step in the **Traffic Light Principle** process that must come into play."

"What's that?" Ben asked.

"This vital step in co-leadership is for both the husband and wife to begin by including God and bringing their request to Him. They **I.O.T.L.** *(inquire of the Lord)* and specifically ask for a red, yellow, or green light. They do not base their light on their feelings, perceptions, experiences, or gender. The Bible offers a great promise: 'If any of you lacks wisdom, let him ask of God, who gives to all generously and without reproach.'[3] God does not give wisdom based on gender. The key step in the **Traffic Light Principle** is to begin with God. A husband and wife individually ask God for wisdom and a specific light, and *then* they wait for unity. Co-leading together like this provides protection from making unwise choices.

"Back to the first married couple—Adam and Eve were in agreement when they ate the forbidden fruit. But they never included God in their process. What if either one of them had asked, 'Father, this serpent says we should eat the fruit from the tree of the knowledge of good and evil You commanded us not to eat. He says You're holding out on us. Is that true?' God would have quickly reminded them what He commanded. If either one of them had asked God for a light, it would have been bright *red*.

"Ben, husband-and-wife unity must go hand in hand with inviting God into the process. Our experience is often that a couple means well and implements the **Traffic Light Principle**. Their focus is on agreement, but they forget to include God.

"Remember our REAL LIFE motto: *marriage is not about me*. That can be expanded to: *it's not about we* (you and your spouse). The wisest advice we can give couples who want to co-lead together is to begin everything with God and process decisions together. First ask God individually, then join together to see first that you are *both* hearing the same thing from God, and second that you *both* have green lights. Only then pull the trigger on your decision. Exercising leadership in unity by including God becomes the pathway to power and protection, as well as increased intimacy in spirit, soul, and body oneness."

Ben replied, "Okay, I see including God is key, but practically speaking, in real life, how do you ever get around to making decisions with all your steps: *inquiring of the Lord* … waiting on God … and waiting for everyone to have green lights?"

Tim said, "Ben, with my personality, temperament, and gift of leadership, there were times as a new follower of Christ early in our marriage where I took charge, made the call on decisions, and expected Anne to joyfully submit to me. Looking back, there was lots of negative fallout in me making the call when we did not have unity with God and each other."

"Can you give me a specific example?" Ben asked.

"I (Anne) will give you a very simple real-life example to highlight the co-leadership *process*."

Life Is Lived in a Story

anne

"When the kids were little, we wanted to get a puppy. We had the money, the kids were excited, I did research on breeders, and we were ready to make the purchase. I casually mentioned to Tim our plans, and he asked me if we should utilize our co-leadership **Traffic Light Principle**. Knowing Tim was an animal lover I said, 'Sure, let's both ask God for a green light.'

"But Tim the animal lover implemented our **I.O.T.L.** principle and came back a few days later and said, 'I know you and the kids are excited about the dog, we have the money, you know I love animals—heck, we've had dozens of pets in our home. Hon, this surprised even me, but when I prayed about it I got a yellow light; not red—not never—but yellow, not now.'

"Let's review how tim+i could have implemented the different marriage views to process our decision to purchase a puppy. First, in the male rulership marriage view, gender trumps. This would mean no dog. Tim, as the ruler in the marriage, would have had authority to make this decision. Second, both the traditional-hierarchical and complementarian marriage views would mean no dog. In the way *head* is traditionally defined Tim would have final authority in making decisions. If he says 'no dog,' gender trumps, so no dog. Third, the egalitarian marriage view could work out in various ways. As a couple we would implement our agreed-upon process. If we had the money, if the kids and I agreed to take care of the dog, and since Tim liked dogs—although Tim had some reservations—according to our agreed-upon process he would submit to me, and I would go ahead and purchase the dog. Or as an egalitarian couple we might agree that taking turns was a top priority in our process. For example, if I made the call on the last family pet, Tim would make the call on this pet decision, because process trumps, and we would not purchase the dog.

"But the way tim+i live out marriage is we co-lead in mutual equality and mutual authority. Our process would be *both* tim+i would **I.O.T.L.** And if we did not *both* have green lights, we would say no dog. *Why?* Because in our marriage unity trumps."

BEN'S LAST QUESTION

Ben appreciated the story, then asked, "Okay, last question: do you use the **Traffic Light Principle** for *every* decision you make?"

Tim told him, "Not every decision. I don't call Anne from the grocery store to see if she has a green light on Red Delicious or Granny Smith apples."

"Then exactly what decisions do you choose *not* to implement the **Traffic Light Principle**?" Ben asked.

"Ben, we are often asked that question, and our response is that a husband and wife can choose not to include God or their spouse in any decision they do not want to include God or their spouse. Remember, a couple doesn't have to walk in togetherness and co-leadership. They get to."

LISTENING FOR GOD'S VOICE

God longs for relationship and intimacy with every man and woman. He created each of us with a need for relationship, with a longing to love and be loved. In *Soul Cravings*, Erwin McManus wrote,

> You were created for relationship. This is and always will be at the core of your being.
>
> All of us have an intrinsic need to belong, and all of us are on a search for intimacy. No matter how many things about us are different, in this we are all the same — we all crave love. It is as if we are searching for a love we have lost. Or perhaps more strangely we are searching for a love we have never known but somehow sense it awaits us.
>
> The most powerful evidence that our souls crave God is that within us there is a longing for love. We are all connected by a thin red line.[4]

The two of us both grew up attending church and believing in God. For the first twenty-two years of our lives we each were connected with a traditional church that emphasized relationship with God the Father. Then as young adults, we fell in love with God the Son. We repented of our sins and entered into relationship with Jesus, purposefully engaging with the Bible and growing in intimacy with Him. In recent years, we've had the joy of becoming more intimately acquainted with God the Holy Spirit, witnessing and personally experiencing His power in our lives.

Along the way, we've learned that growing in intimacy and relationship with God is a lifelong process. It seems as if God just keeps getting bigger and bigger, although it's really our experience of Him that has grown as we have taken deliberate steps to know God better.

Life Is Lived in a Story

anne

In my late twenties I began to actively seek God's heart. I studied my Bible and bought books on spiritual disciplines. These encouraged me to pursue a two-way relationship with God. I began to realize that not only could I talk with God—but He wanted to talk with me too. I was delighted to realize that God wanted to be in an intimate relationship with me. The Hebrews passage came alive to me: "See to it that you do not refuse Him who is speaking."[5]

With a growing family, I needed to start by finding a quiet place. I didn't want anything to distract me. I would pray and wait for God to respond. Sometimes while I was waiting, a spontaneous thought would come to my mind. I would write it in my journal.

As my relationship with God deepened, I began to talk with Him through-out my day. We talked about everything. Over time He became my best friend.

However, learning to hear God's voice created more questions for me. At times I wondered, *What if I am listening to my own voice? What if I think God is speaking, but it is really the voice of others in my head? What if I am hearing the voice of the Enemy? How can I ever be certain that I am hearing from God? Can I know for sure?*

These are all normal questions for anyone who desires to grow in relationship with God. The truth is that a person can hear a number of different voices. They can hear their own voice, the voice of others, the voice of God, or the voice of the Enemy. Answering my concerns, spiritual parents encouraged me to grow in intimacy with God and learn how to discern His voice. I continued to pray, listen, journal, and read God's Word. I noticed that when I spent more time just being with God, it became easier for me to recognize His voice. This is true in every relationship.

For example, my sister-in-law Caryl has two sisters, Lezlie and Jodi. When she and my brother John first began dating, he would often call her at home, but he found it difficult to distinguish Caryl's voice from that of her sisters and her mom, Vera. Since all the female voices sounded the same, John was never quite sure who he was speaking to. He began every conversation by asking the person on the other end of the phone, "Caryl, is that you?" Inevitably the voice on the other end of the phone would reply, "No, it's Lezlie. I'll get Caryl for you."

But as John and Caryl spent more time together, their intimacy grew. Over time John found it easy to distinguish Caryl's voice from her sisters' and her mom's. In fact, eventually he found it hard to believe there was ever a time he did not easily recognize her voice.

So too, as we advance in intimacy with God, as we make it a priority to **I.O.T.L.** *(inquire of the Lord)*, we begin to know Him and recognize His voice. The Bible says that a sheep knows its shepherd's voice. God is the Good Shepherd. He wants us to know and experience Him so intimately that we immediately recognize His voice and distinguish it from the voice of the Enemy or the voices of others.

Distinguishing God's voice from that of others involves an ongoing commitment to growing in intimacy with Him and discerning His heart. Experiencing God personally is one thing—but in marriage, when both a wife and husband together experience God, they will also experience power and protection.

Practically, when either one of us senses God's voice, before acting on it we make sure that we are both in unity with what we are hearing. Since we are in a life long covenant one-flesh relationship, we believe that God will not speak to us in different voices or direct us in opposing ways. When there are differences, as we explained in a previous chapter, we implement the **Traffic Light Principle** and wait until we both have green lights.

For us, as co-leaders we believe *unity trumps disunity*—no matter how much one of us may want what we want. We also make sure that what we are hearing is in agreement with the Bible. We do this because we believe God's voice will never contradict the principles revealed in His Word. Not only do we rely on each other and on God's Word for wisdom and direction, but we also involve other people—those who are more mature in the Lord and can affirm that what we are hearing is in alignment with God's principles.

The Bible is the most widely read book in all of history. For some people, it is their first introduction to God. The pages of the Bible are filled with powerful stories that God uses to draw men and women into relationship with Him, stories that reveal different parts of His nature and character. Not only does the Bible introduce us to God the Son, God the Father, and

God the Holy Spirit, but it gives us a chance to meet ordinary men and women like us who were invited to live extraordinary lives through their relationships with God and in community with others. Reading the Bible with an open heart can be a spiritual experience. Spending time in God's Word is one way to grow in relationship and intimacy with God.

SPIRITUAL DISCIPLINES

There are many ways to deepen your intimacy with God. In addition to listening to God and meditating on His Word, many other spiritual disciplines provide ways to grow in knowing God more intimately. Richard J. Foster, in his book *Celebration of Discipline*, placed spiritual disciplines into three categories.[6] He described the inward disciplines as meditation, prayer, fasting, and study. He referred to the outward disciplines as simplicity, solitude, submission, and service. Finally, he described the corporate disciplines as confession, worship, guidance, and celebration. These spiritual disciplines invite a person into deeper levels of intimacy with God.

The two of us have been in personal relationship with God for most of our lives. For many of those years, if someone asked us if we knew God, we would have confidently answered yes. If we were asked to describe our relationship with God, we would have responded with a list of things we were doing for Him. We went to church, we prayed, we gave our time, talents, and treasures. We tried to do what we thought we were supposed to do in order to show God we loved Him. The problem was, we never knew if we were doing enough, so we kept doing more.

Religion often equates doing things *for* God with being in relationship *with* Him. When a person's major focus is on serving God, it can inhibit their ability to know Him. When doing things for God becomes the priority, God can feel more like a boss than a loving Father. We've come to understand that God enjoys being with a person much more than having him or her do things for Him.

Life Is Lived in a Story

tim

When I took an early retirement from the fire department, we moved from the suburbs of Chicago to Holland, Michigan, where I accepted a full-time pastor's position at a local church. Adjusting to a new home and a new job took time. A seemingly never-ending list of pastoral needs, along with the responsibility of co-leading our family through many major life changes, consumed my energy.

It quickly became apparent that serving God could become the biggest obstacle to my growing in intimacy with Him. During my years as a fireman I could easily schedule time to be with the Lord. But as the needs of our faith community continued to increase, my regular times of just being with the Lord were slowly being replaced with doing lots of good things for Him. I began to feel more like God's employee than His son. As my joy was drained away, I determined to find a way to just be—to hang out—with my good Father.

Down the road from our home on the shores of Lake Michigan was a Christian youth camp that offered area pastors a room for prayer and study at a special daily rate. I decided to rent a room once a month for my DAWG: Day Alone with God. (Yes, I have a thing for acronyms.)

Early one morning I headed downstairs to set out on my first official DAWG. I was all set: in one hand I carried my backpack, cassette player, and cell phone. In the other I gripped my Bible, two books, a notebook, and my daily planner. Anne met me at the door, and as I leaned over to kiss her good-bye, I couldn't help but notice the confused look on her face. "What?" I asked.

"Honey," she said, "where are you going with all of that stuff?"

"Today's my DAWG," I reminded her. "I'm going to Camp Geneva. Why?"

She said, "Well, what if I told you that I really missed you and wanted to spend time with you? What if I rented a room at a camp on the shores of Lake Michigan for an entire day just to be with you?"

In a hurry to kick off my DAWG, I snapped, "What's your point?"

"Well, if I walked into the room and you had your music playing and your Day-Timer out and your books opened and you were busy with a back-pack full of work ... well ... I guess I'd wonder how much you really wanted to be with me."

I looked at Anne, then I looked at all my stuff. Then my wife put her arms around me and said, "Hon, why don't you leave all your stuff at home and just be with your good Father?"

As Anne helped me realize that day, being with God is not about making appointments with Him, although that's not a bad way to get started. Being with God is about spending time in His company, talking with Him, listening to Him, learning to see yourself through His loving eyes.

INQUIRING OF THE LORD: TWELVE PRACTICAL STEPS

We do not have a specific formula or a detailed step-by-step procedure for couples to grow in intimacy with God and their spouse. But we encourage every person to start with God— **I.O.T.L.** *(inquire of the Lord).* Begin by asking God to show you His ways. The Bible says, "You do not have because you do not ask."[7]

Practical steps in growing in intimacy with a spouse can include learning and understanding temperaments, styles of relating, spiritual gifts, and love languages. Understanding these will increase intimacy and help couples advance in their marital "we"— in knowing and being fully known.

Throughout fifty-plus years of going to church, we have listened to thousands of messages. The following are valuable things we've been taught to help us discern what we sense we are hearing and process decisions—*together*.

1. Have you prayed about what you are considering?

Be anxious for nothing, but in everything by prayer and supplication with thanksgiving let your requests be known to God.[8]
Take every thought captive to Christ.[9]

2. Is what you are considering consistent with the principles in the Bible?

He who is spiritual appraises all things.[10]
If any of you lacks wisdom, let him ask of God, who gives to all generously and without reproach.[11]

3. Is what you are considering affirmed by other godly people?

> Where there is no guidance [revelation] the people fall. But in the abundance of counselors there is victory.[12]

4. Will what you are considering bring glory to God?

> Whatever you do in word and deed, do all in the name of the Lord Jesus.[13]

5. Will what you are considering positively impact God's kingdom?

> Seek first His kingdom and His righteousness.[14]
> Remember the kingdom of God has one King (and the king is not the husband).

6. How does what you are considering relate to God's will for your life?

> Rejoice always; pray without ceasing; in everything give thanks; for this is God's will for you in Christ Jesus.[15]

7. Do you have peace about what you are considering?

> And the peace of God, which surpasses all understanding, will guard your hearts and your minds in Christ Jesus.[16]

8. Do you have unity with your spouse (if married)?

> God's original design for marriage included co-leadership in mutual equality and mutual authority where *unity trumps disunity*.[17]

9. Will what you are considering cost you something?

"And He said to them, 'Truly I say to you, there is no one who has left house or wife or brothers or parents or children, for the sake of the kingdom of God, who will not receive many times as much at this time in the age to come, eternal life.'"[18] Remember—cost is not always money; it often it involves servanthood and humility

10. Does what you are considering agree with your life calling and mission?

I therefore ... urge you to walk in a manner worthy of your calling to which you have been called.[19]

Who has called us with a holy calling, not according to our works, but according to His own purpose and grace which was granted us in Christ Jesus.[20]

11. Does what you are considering come from a pure heart?

THE LORD DOES NOT LOOK AT THE THINGS PEOPLE LOOK AT. PEOPLE LOOK AT THE OUTWARD APPEARANCE, BUT THE LORD LOOKS AT THE HEART.[21]
We are never to judge another person's heart; nevertheless, the Bible says, "[The] mouth speaks from that which fills [the] heart."[22]

12. Does what you are considering come from a place of love?

"YOU SHALL LOVE THE LORD YOUR GOD WITH ALL YOUR HEART, AND WITH ALL YOUR SOUL, AND WITH ALL YOUR MIND." This is the great and foremost commandment. The second is like it, "You shall love your neighbor as yourself." On these two commandments depend the whole Law and the Prophets.[23]

The older we get, the more we believe that love is the ball game. The most mature followers of Christ we know throughout our lives are the most loving people we know.

This non-exhaustive list is not based on gender. Notice that each step equally impacts both men and women. Again, in marriage, three keys to co-leading together and making godly decisions are:

1. **I.O.T.L.** *(inquire of the Lord).*
2. Maximize both the husband's and wife's gifts.
3. Wait for unity (until you both have "green lights" from the Lord).

CHAPTER 8

ABSOLUTES AND PREFERENCES

Life Is Lived in a Story

tim+anne

A middle-aged man we will refer to as Jerry approached us at a REAL LIFE Marriage Advance. He appeared a bit upset—almost offended—that we were suggesting it's okay for a husband and wife to prefer co-leadership and mutual authority over his traditional marriage view, which included a marital hierarchy with male authority and the husband as the designated leader.

Jerry declared, "The Bible is crystal clear that a husband has authority over a wife. This is a nonnegotiable marriage absolute!"

We asked, "Help us understand—how do you define an absolute?"

"An absolute is an absolute. It's not compromising on biblical truth. Furthermore, if male leadership in marriage is not an absolute, do you consider *anything* an absolute?"

We replied, "The dictionary defines an absolute as 'completely unequivo-cal and not capable of being viewed as partial or relative.'[1] We believe it's important to know the absolutes, the nonnegotiables in your life and marriage. Jerry, can we write on our whiteboard a few absolutes for you to see?"

"Sure."

The absolutes we put on the board included the quintessential oneness of the Trinitarian God (God the Holy Spirit, God the Son, and God the Father); the birth, life, death, and life-giving resurrection of Jesus Christ; the Great Commandment (love); the Great Commission (go); justification by faith; the authority of Scripture; and the priesthood of all believers. "Jerry," we asked, "as you review our list, are there any of these absolutes that you do *not* agree with?"

Jerry said, "No—I am tracking with you on every one."

We continued. "Jerry, in addition to absolutes, we have preferences. For example, Tim *prefers* ESPN to MSNBC; Anne *prefers* staying home and renting a movie to going to a movie theatre; we both *prefer* Dunkin Donuts coffee to Starbucks; and we both *prefer* hiking in the mountains to working out indoors. Similarly, we have friends who are fully devoted Christ followers who *prefer* many different things."

"Like what?" Jerry asked.

"We have friends who *prefer* contemporary worship to traditional wor-ship; others who *prefer* adult baptism to infant baptism (some *prefer* immersion to sprinkling). Some of our friends *prefer* believing that God still speaks; others say that everything God wants to say to us is written in the Bible. We have friends who *prefer* Wesleyan holiness to Reformed sanctification. Others *prefer* women to be encouraged to use their gifts in all church positions and offices, and some *prefer* women to be restricted in using all the gifts the Holy Spirit has given them solely based on gender. We have friends who *prefer* creationism to evolution. And we have friends who *prefer* Calvinism to Arminianism.[2] Our point is that it's wise to process and determine your *absolutes* and *preferences*."

Jerry said, "Okay, I'll admit that's an interesting perspective on absolutes and preferences, one I've never heard before."

"Jerry, note that every one of the *preferences* we listed can be connected to the Bible. In addition, apart from women using all their gifts in all church offices and positions, none of the other preferences are gender specific or gender exclusive. Nevertheless, as we study Scripture, we discover that throughout the text the writers make building up the church and advancing the kingdom of God top priorities. The Bible commands Christ followers to 'seek *first* the kingdom of God.'"[3]

Jerry asked, "Then help me understand, how does marriage fit into absolutes and preferences?"

"Specifically in regard to marriage, we *prefer* God's original marriage design—co-leadership in mutual equality and mutual authority—over later marriage views that were spawned."

"Can you help me understand what you refer to as marriage views spawned later?" John asked.

"Sure. Married couples can *prefer* certain interpretations of a handful of debated New Testament marriage texts. This results in couples preferring to live out different marriage views—all of which surfaced *after* sin entered the marriage story. We refer to these marriage views as: the male rulership marriage view—'your desire shall be for your husband and he shall rule over you'[4]; the traditional-hierarchical-complementarian marriage views; and the egalitarian marriage view. In our marriage we prefer to try to live out God's original marriage design—the design from *before* sin entered the story. This includes mutual equality, mutual authority, and co-leadership."

"How can couples live out God's original marriage design?" Jerry asked.

We replied, "God—Jesus Christ—coming to earth in human form and taking back dominion from Satan has enabled couples to reclaim co-leadership. Men and women in the power of God have the ability to resist the Devil. It is written, 'Submit therefore to God. Resist the devil and he will flee from you. Draw near to God and He will draw near to you.'[5] By grace, dominion and co-leadership can be reclaimed: 'For sin shall not have dominion over you, for you are not under law but under grace.'[6]

"In addition, as men and women truly understand that they are sons and daughters of a good God, they can step into their true identity individually and together as couples. This can provide limitless opportunities to advance God's kingdom. **Rulership** regained enables women and men to overcome the god of this world. 'Greater is He who is in you than he who is in the world.'[7] This becomes the pathway for couples to choose God's original marriage principles and co-lead together."

Jerry told us, "I've gone to church my entire life—I've taken seminary classes and have studied the Bible for years; it's where I base my theology.[8] It seems to me that what you are saying about marriage ... I don't know, so much of this is new to me. In fact, if what you're saying is truly in the Bible, then why wouldn't it be taught in churches and seminaries? I guess the bottom line I default to is if it's not clearly spelled out in the Bible, I'm not buying it!"

"Jerry, we used to make that exact same statement; truth be told, we prided ourselves in regularly declaring, 'If it's not in the Bible, we don't believe it.' But specifically in regard to marriage, we believe God's original design and principles for co-leadership in marriage are described in Genesis before the fall. However, as far as your 'it must be spelled out in my Bible' comment, we personally no longer make that statement."

"Why?"

"Because there are a number of things we believe that we cannot find specifically spelled out in the Bible."

"Can you give me an example?"

"Yes. We've been involved in youth ministry for decades; we believe it's a key ministry in many churches. However, local church youth ministry as it currently operates in most churches—where is that specifically addressed in the Bible?"

"Youth ministry is in the Bible," Jerry replied.

"Please give us the exact chapter and verse; we can't find it. We see the Bible placing spiritual formation of children and adolescents as the primary responsibility of the parents and family, not a local church pastor or children-youth ministry.

"There are other things we don't find in the Bible. For example, Sunday worship is not commanded in the Bible, and we don't find the term *holy Bible* in the Bible. Furthermore, we have used the sinner's prayer many times to help share the gospel, but we do not find the sinner's prayer specifically quoted in the Bible. One more example: the holy Trinity of God is an absolute for us, yet we do not find *holy Trinity* in the Bible. Nevertheless, we support youth ministry and Sunday worship, we love the holy Bible, we continue to use the sinner's prayer, and we believe one hundred percent in the Trinity of God. But for us to take what we now consider a hyper-legalistic approach and require everything we believe to be specifically spelled out in jot-and-tittle detail—to us that's unwise."

Jerry said, "But you have to understand, as a lifelong evangelical, I just hold to certain tenets of the faith with absolutely no exceptions."

"Can you give us one example?" we asked.

"Well, I'm not asked questions like that very often, but a bottom-line truth for me is that a person must be in a personal relationship with Jesus."

"Jerry, show us where a personal relationship with Jesus is in the Bible. Will you please give us the exact chapter and verse?"

"It's in the Gospels."

"Exactly which gospel?"

"I'm not sure, but I'm certain it's in one of them; come on—are you messing with me? You know that a personal relationship with Jesus is what life is all about."

"Well, how about we take a short break, and you can look up that passage and get back to us?"

"We don't need to take a break; it will take only a minute to find that passage because I have a Bible on my phone."

"Great."

"Okay, I will type in *personal relationship with Jesus*. I'll start with the New American Standard Bible ... hmmm, that's interesting, it says no results found. I'll try NIV Bible ... same response—no results found. I'll try *The Message* ... it says no results found. It's probably in the Amplified Bible ... same response: no results found. Wait ... I'll try the King James Bible ... this is amazing, it says no results found. One more—I'll try the New King James Bible ... it also says no results found. I wonder if my phone Bible is broken."

"Jerry, we don't think your phone Bible is broken. We've never found that what you say is a basic tenant of faith—a bottom-line truth of a personal relationship with Jesus in any Bible ."

"Frankly I'm shocked that a personal relationship with Jesus is not in the Bible."

We reminded him, "Remember, Jesus never made a personal relationship with Him the end-all, be-all. In fact Jesus said, 'But I tell you the truth, it is to your advantage that I go away; for if I do not go away; the Helper will not come to you; but if I go, I will send Him to you.'[9] It appears Jesus emphasized that an intimate relationship with the Holy Spirit trumped a personal relationship with Him.

"Jerry, hear our hearts—we each have a personal relationship with Jesus; it's a cornerstone of our stories. But the truth is *personal relationship with Jesus* is not in any Bible we are aware of. Over the years we have found that sincere followers of Jesus Christ can hold dearly to what they call bottom-line absolute truths. Yet they often have trouble connecting their bottom-line absolute truths to a particular verse in the Bible.

"Specifically in regard to marriage, scholars, theologians, and church leaders use different biblical methods of interpretation and reach a number of different fallible interpretations for the handful of marriage texts on headship and submission.[10]

"That is why we prefer to get our theology for marriage from God's original marriage principles ... from before sin entered the story and other marriage views—male rulership, traditional-hierarchical, complementarian, egalitarian—were spawned."

Jerry asked, "What other things might we take for granted as being in the Bible?"

"Well, we've already mentioned youth ministry, Sunday worship, the words *holy Bible*, the sinner's prayer, specific references to the Trinity of God, and a personal relationship with Jesus. And we have never found mention of Evangelical, Roman Catholic, Eastern Orthodox, Protestant, Presbyterian, Reformed, Arminian, Lutheran, Wesleyan, Pentecostalism, Charismatic, Apostolic, Congregationalists, Baptists, Anabaptists, Methodist, Episcopalian, Anglican, Foursquare, or other specific church denominations in our Bibles. Neither have we found the terms dispensationalism, Christian Zionism, Calvinism, Wesleyan holiness, Arminianism, Reformed theology, or even Protestant evangelism specifically spelled out in our

Bibles. Yet our experience is that men and women—especially religious leaders—have very strong opinions and feelings about every one of these.

"Jerry, back to absolutes and preferences: we prefer living in the Larger Story where God is the main character and *it's not about me* rather than living in the smaller story where I am the main character and *it's all about me*. In marriage we prefer God's original design of co-leading together rather than male rulership, traditional-hierarchical-complementarian, or egalitarian marriage views. In order for a couple to co-lead together and live out God's original marriage design, they must understand the importance of mutual equality—*both* made in the image of God—and mutual authority—*both* given the dominion and procreation mandates. This involves being mutually dependent: first on God, and then interdependent on each other. The heart of marriage—of two becoming one—involves a mystery we will never fully understand. But that doesn't mean we can't keep trying.

CHAPTER 9

EQUALITY, HEADSHIP, SUBMISSION, AND AUTHORITY

God's original co-leadership marriage design is not taught in most churches and seminaries. We believe that this is primarily because of a handful of controversial New Testament marriage texts. People with strong opinions claim that their interpretation is the correct, biblical, factual, only-way-to-view-marriage perspective. Numerous books and blogs have endlessly debated these issues.

So while our focus is God's original marriage design, we want to take one chapter to briefly look at equality, headship, submission, and authority.

EQUALITY

People with different marriage perspectives (male rulership, traditional-hierarchical-complementarian, and egalitarian) all agree that both men and women are made in the image of God—they are *intrinsically equal*. However, male rulership and traditional-hierarchical-complementarian proponents would say men and women are not *functionally equal*.

Egalitarian marriage proponents would align with God's original marriage design. They believe men and women are *intrinsically equal* (both made in God's image) and *functionally equal* because in the beginning both the man and woman were given the dominion and procreation mandates.

HEADSHIP

Headship can often become a divisive issue in marriage discussions—especially in religious circles. Various "infallible" headship interpretations and accompanying dialogue could fill a library. Our experience is that people will endlessly argue the original Greek and Hebrew, lexicons, grammar roots, verb tenses, hermeneutical and eschatological anthropomorphisms, and endless jots and tittles until Jesus Christ returns.

Our preference is to invest our time and energy focusing on God's original co-leadership marriage principles. We are not theologians. But for decades, we've studied different headship interpretations. Our understanding is that proponents of the male rulership and traditional-hierarchical-complementarian marriage views interpret headship as meaning that the husband is the head (*kephale*) who has authority over the wife. Egalitarian marriage view proponents believe headship means "source"—as in headwaters.

Theologian Dr. Gilbert Bilezikian added:

> It is often assumed that "head" in the Koine Greek of the New Testament, means leader, boss or authority. However, despite the fact that there are scores of references with all kinds of titles to leaders in every area of life in the New Testament, none is ever designated as "head." The word "head" used in this manner appears exclusively

in the relation of Christ to the church paralleled in that of husband to wife. In each of those New Testament references, the function of Christ's headship to the church is one of servant-provider and never one of authority or leadership.[1]

As you can see, the scholarly debate about headship can get pretty "heady." Our position is that before sin entered the picture, there was no designated hierarchy, headship, or female subordination, and man was not declared the leader or spiritual cover. Headship is never mentioned until thousands of years after God's original marriage design. In Eden the husband and wife enjoyed mutual equality intrinsically and functionally. The husband and wife co-led together—naked and not ashamed—as they celebrated the miracle and mystery of two becoming one.

The Bible has a little over 31,000 verses, but it isn't until Ephesians 5:23 that the apostle Paul—for the first time in all of history—described the husband as the head (*kephale*) of his wife. This makes us wonder: *if headship is a foundational component in the husband/wife relationship, doesn't it make sense that Jesus would have made it a key point—an absolute—when He talked about marriage?* But Jesus never mentioned headship. In fact, when Jesus talked about marriage, He returned to the one-flesh togetherness principles of Eden.[2]

Nevertheless, we understand that many men and women consider headship a major marriage focus. When this is the case, we encourage the husband to act as the head as the Ephesians passage describes. The husband is to love his wife 'as Christ also loved the church.'[3] How did Christ love the church? He 'gave Himself up for her,'[4] 'nourish[ing] and cherish[ing]' her.[5] As head, Christ died for the church; likewise a husband as head is to give himself up for—nourish, cherish, love, serve, and be willing to die for—his bride. For the record, we have no problem with husbands living out headship in those ways.

Our experience is that walking out headship differs from couple to couple. Most religious leaders (including male rulership and traditional-hierarchical-complementarian marriage-view proponents) believe that headship means the husband has functional authority—and unless something is immoral or illegal—the right to have the final say in making decisions. It's like the husband possesses a gender trump card. Essentially there is a functional hierarchy with the husband first and the wife second.

Personally we have concerns with interpretations in which *head* means the husband has final say and, if necessary, is able to impose his decision on his spouse. *Impose* is defined as "insist on something, make people agree or comply."[6] No where in Scripture does it say a husband has the position or the authority to force his wife to submit to him.

Throughout church history the "Christ as head of the church" metaphor has been misinterpreted, misunderstood, and misapplied. As we look to Jesus as our model for headship, do we see Jesus ever having final say in making decisions? Does Jesus ever pull out a trump card and impose His will or make people comply? For example, does Jesus ever impose His desire for a person to avoid sin, repent, pray, serve at church, tithe, or live in certain ways?

For that reason, we do not agree with marriage views (male rulership and traditional-hierarchical-complementarian) where the husband has final say in making decisions or, figuratively speaking, has a male gender trump card.

Reread the Ephesians text. We believe the heart of headship includes an invitation to step into the Larger Story where God is the main character, and to not live in the smaller story where functionally the husband is the main character. Biblical headship includes a husband denying himself, dying to selfishness, and placing his spouse's needs and feelings above his own. Remember, these commands to husbands in that season of history were so over-the-top countercultural. At that time, life was all about men, and women were treated as property—having a wife was similar to owning an animal.

In addition, we find most male rulership and traditional-hierarchical-complementarian marriage proponents believe that as part of his headship role the husband is also the wife's spiritual cover. Practically, this means a wife goes through her husband in the decision-making process because, as head, he is the spiritual leader in marriage. We do not believe this lines up with Scripture: "For there is one God and one mediator between God and [human]kind, the man Christ Jesus."[7] Our humble opinion is men and women—husbands and wives—are to go directly to Jesus Christ; they are not to first go through any person—spouse, saint, or religious leader.

SUBMISSION

Submission in marriage often comes with lots of negative baggage. In fact, many people refer to submission as the S-word. Let's review the Apostle Paul's letter to the church in Ephesus. He begins Ephesians chapter 5 talking about walking in love;[8] then the dangers of immorality and impurity;[9] filthiness and silly talk;[10] idolatry;[11] deception and empty words;[12] darkness and light;[13] wisdom;[14] spirit filled living;[15] worshipping the Lord;[16] and always giving thanks[17]. It appears there was a lot going on in Ephesus that Paul addressed before he talked about marriage.

As far as submission, in Ephesians chapter 5 Paul stated a previously unheard-of, culture-shattering command. He introduced a revolutionary New Testament concept that focused on *mutual* submission: "be subject to one another in the fear of Christ."[18] Note that this other-centered command was not only for husbands and wives but for *all* followers of Christ. In the next verse Paul stated; "Wives *be subject* to your own husbands, as to the Lord."[19] It is important to note that the words *be subject* are written in italics indicating they are not found in the original text. Literally verse 22 reads, "Wives to their own husbands as to the Lord." Unfortunately, the New International Version and many other translations don't make note of this. It is also important to note that no where in this passage is a wife commanded to submit to the authority of her husband. Our experience is often traditional-hierarchical-complementarian marriage proponents automatically connect submission to authority.

The reality is that there are only a few Bible texts that focus on submission in marriage. One passages is in the Apostle Peter's Epistle where he instructed a wife to be submissive to her husband.[20] Similar to the Ephesians passage that focused on mutual submission,[21] Bible interpreters often pay little attention when Peter stated "In the same way"[22] and "You husbands likewise".[23] These commands highlighted mutuality and mutual submission between a husband and wife. Re-read Peter's pastoral letter, his overall theme was not about submission, but "the true grace of God"[24] in the life of every believer.

We understand that men and women who support traditional-hierarchical-complementarian marriage views that include functional male authority often ask people with a mutual authority marriage position (egalitarian and God's original design marriage views) to cite a Bible verse where a husband is commanded to submit to his wife. The response of mutual authority proponents is typically Ephesians 5:21, which clearly commands *every* person to "be subject to one another in the fear of Christ." These people believe "one another" includes husbands and wives. But the truth is that there is no biblical command that specifically says, "Husbands submit to wives."

However, we believe the mutual submission commanded to all Christ followers in Ephesians 5:21 includes husbands, wives, and single men and women. Furthermore, there are many *one another* and *each other* passages in the Bible. For example, in the gospel of John, Jesus addresses *both* men and women with a new command "that you also love *one another.*"[25] Galatians 5:13 says, "Through love serve *one another.*" Ephesians 4:32 says, "Be kind to *one another.*" Romans 12:10 says, "Be devoted to *one another;* ... give preference to *one another.*" Philippians 2:3 says, "Do nothing from selfishness or empty conceit, but with humility of mind regard *one another* as more important than yourselves." From these examples it is clear that the phrase *one another* applies to both men and women. Therefore, why would the command to "be subject to *one another*" in Ephesians 5:21, which precedes marriage instructions, be any different?

Reviewing these and many other *one another* texts, none are gender exclusive. Nevertheless, if a person takes what we consider a hyper-legalistic approach based on the position that husbands are not specifically commanded to submit to wives, our response is to ask them to cite an exact book, chapter, and verse that commands "do not smoke cigarettes" or "do not shoot heroin." Everyone agrees these are important components to living a healthy lifestyle, yet they are not specifically commanded in the Bible.

Therefore, it is unwise for a person to build their theology based on the silence of Scripture. The fact that the Bible does not command a husband to submit to his wife should not open the door to build a case for male hierarchy, male leadership, or female subordination. Especially in light of the passages that command mutual submission[26] and mutual authority,[27] as well as the over fifty *one another* and *each other* passages that clearly apply to *all* men and women—many of whom are husbands and wives.

Ephesians 5 is a text that many people base much of their traditional-hierarchical-complementarian marriage theology on. The apostle Paul understood authority and hierarchy; if he wanted, he could have clearly designated a hierarchy where the man had authority over his wife. In fact, in the first verse of the next chapter Paul commanded, "Children, obey your parents."[28] Likewise, Paul could have easily commanded, "Wives, obey your husbands," but he didn't. Instead he introduced to a male rulership culture a new, revolutionary marriage view of mutual submission.[29] And a new concept of headship where the husband was commanded to nourish, cherish, and be willing to die for his wife.

It's also interesting to note that, at the end of Ephesians 5, the apostle Paul went back to the beginning. He returned to God's original marriage principles and quoted Genesis 2:24: "For this cause a man shall leave his father and mother, and shall cleave to his wife; and the two shall become one flesh."[30]

In Ephesians 5, Spirit-filled mutual submission[31] is the central principle that is then applied in slightly different ways to husbands and wives in a marriage relationship.[32] God's overall theme for life as well as for marriage is mutual submission and reciprocal servanthood. Rather than placing an inordinate focus on submission—even mutual submission—we focus on love. The reality is that it's possible to submit without love, but it's impossible to love without submitting. Bottom line, after all is said and done, *love is the ball game.*

AUTHORITY

We believe authority is at the heart of much marriage misunderstanding and debate. Most interpretations and discussions surrounding headship and submission relate to authority. Over the years traditional-hierarchical-complementarian marriage-view proponents have described their perceived authority in different ways. Some husbands have told us that as the leader they have a 51 percent role in making decisions and the wife has 49 percent. As we listen to these men explain their marriage, we can't help but wonder, *How is a 51/49 functional authority any different from a husband who has 99 percent authority and a wife who has 1 percent?* Either way, the husband has final authority to make decisions.

Other husbands describe their authority as being *the first among equals*. Frankly, this interpretation of God's design for marriage seems confusing to us. Our initial question to couples who live marriage this way is, what does *first among equals* mean? It seems to us that if a husband is *first*, that means his wife is *second*. The words *first* and *second* do not describe mutual equality and mutual authority—the co-leadership we believe God designed for marriage.

We've also heard husbands say somewhat tongue in cheek, "As the leader, I have authority to make all the *major* decisions in my marriage, but after decades of marriage, we've never had one *major* decision." This position seems to indicate to us that the husband is abdicating responsibility in his perceived authority role. Or the husband does not recognize his wife as having mutual authority.

In addition, there are those who try to establish a hierarchical authority structure of man over woman. They often use 1 Corinthians 11:3 to try to support their position. This is a text that is endlessly debated. Let's review what theologian Dr. Gilbert Bilezikian says:

> The text in 1 Corinthians 11:3 is often cited as establishing a top-down hierarchy:
>
> *God over Christ—Christ over man—man over woman.*
>
> However, this biblical text must be radically dismembered and its components reshuffled to produce such results. The untouched biblical sequence is totally different, and it does not present a hierarchical structure:
>
> *Christ, head of man—man, head of woman—God, head of Christ.*
>
> The teaching in this text concerns the concept of "head" as giver of life. In creation, Christ (as the Word, John 1:3) gave life to the man; man to woman (as she was taken from him, Gen. 2:21-23); and in the incarnation, God gave life to Christ (Luke 1:35). This understanding of "head" as "provider of life" is consistent with the immediate context, which deals with the significance of origination (1 Cor. 11:7-12).[33]

Other traditional-hierarchical-complementarian marriage proponents claim that the reference in 1 Peter 3 to Sarah obeying Abraham establishes a marital hierarchy. Remember, the apostle Paul wrote that statement fully aware that Abraham obeyed Sarah multiple times. For example, God instructed Abraham that "whatever Sarah tells you, listen to her."[34] Furthermore, it's very interesting to us that in regard to authority in marriage, the only time authority between a husband and wife is specifically mentioned is in 1 Corinthians 7:4: "The wife does not have *authority* over her own body, but the husband does; and likewise also the husband does not have *authority* over his own body, but the wife does." The Bible clearly commands *mutual authority* to both the husband and wife.[35]

Bottom line, couples can choose different marriage views that came after sin (male rulership, traditional-hierarchical-complementarian, and egalitarian) as well as interpretations of equality, headship, submission, and authority. Our encouragement is for couples with teachable hearts and open minds to explore marriage texts and personal marriage views based on God's original marriage design before sin. This includes mutual equality and mutual authority. Co-leading together: **reflecting**, **revealing**, **ruling**, and **reproducing**.

As we survey our culture and the current marriage landscape, we sense God inviting men and women (husbands and wives) not to focus on who has authority or to debate the precise meaning of *head*, but rather to focus on walking in humility—loving, serving, and together advancing God's kingdom.

Life Is Lived in a Story

tim+anne

At a REAL LIFE marriage gathering, a man we will refer to as Marvin approached us and said, "I am struggling with your co-leadership marriage position. I've been married for forty years, and as the man—as a seasoned church elder—you might say I'm traditional or hierarchical, but I enjoy being the leader and providing a spiritual cover over my wife. In fact, I've been a successful leader throughout my entire life. In all honesty, I like being the person in charge. Furthermore, as I review a lifetime of personal and professional experiences, I believe that every organization and team needs a leader. In marriage there has to be one person who is the designated leader and who is in charge—and in my marriage that's me."

Marvin continued, "I like my traditional interpretations and applications of equality, headship, submission, and authority. I believe as a husband—as the head—I have authority over my wife. As far as submission goes, the Bible is clear: one of my wife's primary roles is that she submits to me.

"However, I don't want you getting the wrong idea when I say I like having authority—having the final say in my marriage. Therefore, can I give you a word picture that pretty much sums up how my wife and I walk out our marriage?"

"Sure," we told him.

"In our marriage I am the pilot and my wife is my copilot. Certainly we are flying together. But I am the one who decides our direction, speed, and when and where we take off and land. I don't consider myself a bossy pilot. In fact I make it a point to regularly check in with my wife. But I am the pilot. As the husband I am ultimately responsible for our marital journey together."

We said, "We think we understand your marriage illustration. You are the pilot, the leader—the person in charge. Is that correct?"

"Yes, but I'm not a hyper-religious, controlling type of pilot. I regularly ask for my wife's input, and we decide on destinations together. And for the record, I even let my wife take the controls once in a while. Frankly, my traditional marriage view has worked for thousands of years. Help me understand what's wrong with this view."

We responded, "First, it's important to remember that the way a couple lives out marriage is a *preference*, not a salvation or eternal-life issue. Marvin, we recognize and respect your marriage preference and that you have been a successful leader throughout your life.

"In addition, we believe that a person in charge is important in families, in churches, in the business world, in the military, and on sports teams. For example, every family needs parents, church members need leaders, a country needs a leader, a business needs a CEO, the military needs a general, and a sports team needs a captain."

"That's right!" Marvin interjected.

"But unlike families, churches, politics, businesses, the military, and sports teams, we believe God purposely designed marriage to be different. Marriage is unique and unlike any other relationship. In marriage God created *both* the husband and wife to **reflect** and **reveal** His plurality and nature. In the Trinity of God there is no hierarchy. No part of the Godhead is designated president, CEO, general, or captain. One of the extraordinary components of the miracle and mystery of marriage is that, unlike every other relationship, marriage is the only relationship where God invites a man and woman to 'become one.' Together in spirit, soul, and body, a husband and wife co-lead in unity and servanthood—"

Marvin interrupted, "But in my marriage I am the pilot. Someone *must* be in control!"

We replied, "Marvin, let's use your flying illustration. In our marriage God is the pilot, and we are His co-pilots. Our focus is living out God's original marriage principles. This includes co-leading together in mutual equality and mutual authority as *both* of us choose to give up control to God.

"Marvin, for the record, as we grow in living our marriage with God in charge and at the controls, God has taken us on adventures in marital oneness and intimacy that neither one of us could ever have imagined in our wildest dreams."

Marvin shook his head, took a deep breath, and asked, "But how do you two do that?"

We paused before answering. "Marvin, we love this quote by Thomas Merton: 'A prophet isn't someone who tells a slave he should be free, but someone who tells those who think they are free that they are slaves.' Our experience is that male rulership and traditional-hierarchical-complementarian marriage proponents believe the husband has functional authority. And he can choose to exercise his perceived authority in the decision-making process. But stop and think about this: how much authority does a husband really have in a one-flesh lifelong marriage relationship? Bottom line, authority often leads to control, and control responds to control. Similarly, love responds to love, and love lasts forever.[36]

"Throughout the past three decades, we've counseled hundreds of couples, exploring authority, headship, and submission and reviewing the biblical commands for the husband—as head—to nourish, cherish, and be willing to die for his wife.[37] Our real-life experience is this may work fine for some couples when things are going well. But when chaos surfaces and the going gets tough, or when couples reach a logjam, many husbands revert to what they've been taught by religious leaders: that headship includes a functional hierarchy with the husband over the wife. Male rulership, traditional-hierarchical-complementarian marriage proponents often infallibly interpret a handful of marriage texts and reach the conclusion that—unless something is immoral or illegal—a husband has authority to compel his wife to submit to him in the decision-making process.

"Nevertheless, no matter what marriage label (male rulership, traditional-hierarchical-complementarian) is used, stop and soberly evaluate the current state of marriage. How many Christian couples do you know whose marriages are thriving and who *together* are passionately and purposefully advancing God's kingdom?"

Marvin said, "I've never been asked that question. In all honesty, I guess there are not that many couples I personally know whose marriages are passionately and purposefully advancing God's kingdom."

"Marvin, as we've looked into the eyes of more wives than we can count, and reviewing Thomas Merton's words, we wonder: might husbands who define headship in a way that includes male authority and the husband having the final say ... might they unknowingly be slaves to the authority and control they think they have? Is it possible that many husbands are missing out on the power and protection—the kingdom-advancing potential—available in a marriage that includes co-leadership in mutual equality and mutual authority?

"Furthermore, might wives who define headship in ways that include male authority and the husband having the final say ... might they unknowingly be slaves to the functional inequality and hierarchy in their marriage model? Is it possible many wives are missing out on the power and protection—the kingdom-advancing potential—available in a marriage that includes co-leadership in mutual equality and mutual authority?"

Marvin replied, "Okay, but who has the final say in your marriage?"

"After thirty-eight years of marriage, we try *not* to focus on who has authority, who's in control, or who has the final say. Instead we focus on what we believe is right. For us, rightness in marriage includes God's original marriage design of mutual equality and mutual authority. We both passionately work at living out spirit-soul-body oneness. And our primary focus is not on headship-submission-authority, but on loving and serving God and each other—*together*—as co-leaders."

CHAPTER 10

LOVE, RESPECT, AND ROLES

Life Is Lived in a Story

tim

At a REAL LIFE Marriage Advance, a middle-aged married man we will refer to as Joe asked me, "Don't you think that in addition to the obvious anatomical differences, the differences between husbands and wives are pretty clear?"

I replied, "Joe, will you please explain the clear differences to us?"

"I've been taught that as a husband, I am the leader, the initiator, and the spiritual cover over my wife."

"It sounds like you live your marriage in the traditional-hierarchical marriage view, is that right?"

"Well, actually I prefer calling my marriage model complementarianism—this means my wife, as a woman, complements me. And as a husband, I complement my wife."

"Joe, I've heard the word *complementarian* used in marriage discussions. However, when I looked it up in the dictionary, the word wasn't there. My sense is that men who disliked being called traditional or hierarchists invented the word. Nevertheless, we find the word *complementarian* is used with a number of variations, including *complementarian, comple-mentarian with hierarchy*, and *soft complementarian.* Egalitarians often use the term *complementarian* and add *without hierarchy*. However, no matter what new words are invented, in male rulership and traditional-hierarchical-complementarian marriages, the husband has functional authority over the wife. Egalitarian marriages are more in line with our pre-fall marriage position of mutual authority. Joe, no matter what you call your marriage preference, how is it walked out?"

Joe explained, "I guess what I'm saying is I am the leader—hopefully a man's man who is supposed to wear the pants in the family. And my wife is designed to be more gentle and humble in heart."

"Joe, how does that practically play out in real life?"

Joe said, "A wife is supposed to submit, support, and be sensitive to her husband. Husbands are the leaders and teachers. In Paul's letter to Timothy, the Bible describes how women are supposed to 'quietly receive instruction with entire submissiveness.'[1] Paul also instructed women not 'to teach or exercise authority over a man, but to remain quiet.'"[2]

"Joe, that is a text scholars continue to debate. Godly Christ followers have reached a number of 'infallible' interpretations surrounding those passages."

Joe responded, "But the Bible says what it says. Please help me understand your take on that passage."

"Joe, in that text rather than using common Greek words for authority, like exousia or proistemo, the Apostle Paul used a unique word—authentein. This word is used only one time in the entire Bible which makes it very difficult to determine the exact meaning. Many scholars believe authentein means 'to dominate, to usurp authority' or 'don't teach in a domineering way'. They believe Paul was addressing a specific domineering and rebellious woman that Timothy had written to him about. Furthermore, many scholars believe when the Apostle Paul said 'I do not permit'[3] that this is more accurately interpreted as 'I am not currently permitting'. In this specific situation, not permitting one domineering woman—and that is singular: one woman—in one church, Ephesus, in the early season of Christianity to teach because of all the chaos going on in that church. Similar to the cultural commands regarding dress codes for women[4], or Paul's statement preceding this one where he addressed men and said; 'I want men everywhere to lift up holy hands in prayer'[5] These prohibitions and commands were not universal for all churches, for all men and women, for all of history.

"Joe, in regard to your position that restricts women from exercising all the spiritual gifts God gave them, stop and consider this fact: throughout the Bible we see women not being silenced but passionately engaging in ministry. For example, the apostle Paul addressed women who pray and prophesy.[6] And at the end of Paul's letter to the church in Rome, he honored more women than men.[7] He affirmed women's authority as ministers of the gospel. A few of the women Paul honored include Phoebe, a church deacon;[8] Prisca, a fellow worker;[9] Mary;[10] and Junias, who Paul said was 'outstanding among the apostles.'[11]

"Joe, be careful when you use selective literalism and apply this Timothy passage to all women in all churches for all time."

"What do you mean by selective literalism?" Joe asked.

"Selective literalism," I said, "is picking a certain text and 'infallibly' interpreting it one way, and then when a similar statement is made somewhere else, 'infallibly' interpreting it another way. For example, do you take the same position about silence when you interpret the passage in Titus where the apostle Paul said, 'There are many rebellious men ... who must be silenced'?[12] Remember, that command was directed to a specific group of men; it was not a universal command for every rebellious man—which would include all men for all time. All that is to say—Joe, please help me understand your comment about women being required to remain quiet in church."

"Okay," Joe said, "I guess what I'm saying is women can speak in church. But your point about selective literalism is interesting. Tim, can you give me another example of selective literalism?"

I nodded. "I'll try. The Bible commands followers of Christ to greet one another in a very specific way. Multiple times the Bible clearly instructs Christians to greet one another with a holy kiss.[13] Joe, if we met at church, would you obey this clear biblical command and greet me with a holy kiss?"

Joe said, "No, in our culture we don't take 'greet one another with a holy kiss' literally."

I asked him, "But help me understand—how can a person so easily dismiss the repeated biblical commands to greet one another with a holy kiss based on the culture when that command was written. And then when it comes to marriage, using one example, interpret *head* in Ephesians 5 to mean the husband having authority, absolutize it, and create a universal doctrine in regard to how all Christian husbands and wives are to relate for all time? Especially when their interpretation opposes the mutual equality and mutual authority God originally designed for marriage, as well as the mutual authority clearly commanded to both husbands and wives in 1 Corinthians 7 and the reciprocal servanthood commanded to both men and women in Philippians 2:3?

LOVE AND RESPECT

Joe continued, "Thanks, Tim—I'm beginning to understand the implications and dangers of using selective literalism and not taking culture into consideration. But can we get back to marriage?"

"Sure," I responded.

"Hopefully this will clarify and help you better understand the way I walk out my marriage. Bottom line, I am to love my wife and my wife is to respect me. The Bible clearly states this at the end of Ephesians 5. A husband must love his wife as he loves himself, and the wife must respect her husband. Tim, this text is *crystal clear!*"

"Joe, I'm familiar with that unique and one-of-a-kind short passage, but throughout Scripture, *both* husbands and wives are created to love and be loved. In fact, the passage you just quoted says a husband must love his wife as he loves himself. Seems to me it's *crystal clear* that love is important to husbands—beginning with self love. Furthermore, Jesus summed up the entire Law and the Prophets with what has become known as the Great Commandment: to love God, love our neighbors, and love ourselves.[14] Love is the primary goal for both husbands and wives—for all Christ followers. In the well-known love passage written to the church in Corinth the apostle Paul declared: 'And yet I will show you the most excellent way'[15]—the way of love. He concluded this famous chapter with 'and now these three remain; faith, hope, and love. But the greatest of these is love.'"[16]

"But every husband needs respect!" Joe told me.

"Joe, love and respect are not gender exclusive. In 1 Peter 3:7, husbands are commanded to grant a wife honor as a fellow heir of the grace of life. Honor and respect go hand in hand; the Bible commands the wife to respect her husband and the husband to honor his wife as a fellow heir. The Bible also states that 'marriage is to be held in honor among all.'[17] In addition to a wife respecting her husband, in Titus 2:4 wives are to 'love their husbands.' This illuminates the oneness, intimacy, and co-leadership unique to marriage. Joe, can I ask you a question?"

"Sure."

"Looking at the life of Jesus Christ, do you think He focused more on love or respect?"

Joe slowly said, "I'm not sure."

"We read that after Jesus's death and resurrection, He was preparing a meal for Peter, one of His closest friends. Remember that before Jesus's crucifixion Peter denied Jesus three times. The Bible describes how the resurrected Christ asked Peter three times, 'Do you *love* Me?'[18] It's interesting to note that Jesus did not ask Peter, 'Do you *respect* Me?' Jesus understood the transforming power of love in the heart and life of a man. He understood that love, not respect, lasts forever."

Joe responded, "Tim, read the text—the Ephesians passage commands a wife to *respect her husband*."

"Joe, to overemphasize respect for men leads to deemphasizing respect for women. Think about this: a person cannot love without committing to the valuing that love entails. Recognizing value in another person is foundational to respect. A person can respect without loving. For example, in the fire department a firefighter was required to respect a fire officer because of that person's rank—not required to love the officer. Likewise, a wife can respect her husband without loving him. However, it's impossible to love without respecting because respect is one of the necessary ingredients of love."

Joe responded, "But the love-and-respect marriage message is so popular."

I replied, "Joe, our experience is that popular messages can often take on a life of their own. We have husbands come into our counseling office describing to us how they are convinced the major problem in their marriage is that their wives do not give them the respect the Bible commands—and they deserve. Amazingly, it rarely crosses their male minds that their marriage problems could relate to their own selfishness, family-of-origin issues, co-dependency, control, rebellion, rejection, or choice to live in the smaller story where *it's all about me*.

"Joe, as we have invested in exploring love-and-respect principles, we've advanced in our own marriage. But after decades of counseling, we have determined that a healthy, kingdom-advancing marriage is much more than a husband focusing on love and a wife focusing on respect. Marriage is not that simple; intimate relationships are complex."

Joe asked, "Can you give me a love-and-respect example from your life?"

"I'll try. I remember a time when I was disrespectful to Anne in a major way. During the week, something funny had happened to her. That weekend we were driving to a firemen's party, and on our way she looked me directly in the eyes and told me she did *not* want me to share what had happened to her because it would be embarrassing. I promised not to tell the story, even though it was hilarious. Firemen's parties are always filled with great food, tons of fun, and lots of cold beverages. As the night progressed, I forgot my promise to Anne and shared with some firemen the story about her. When she overheard me telling the story, she became angry. On the drive home she explained to me how disrespectful and discounting my behavior was, and how my not keeping my promise inhibited her from trusting that I would do what I said I would do.

"When we got home I looked her in her eyes and told her I was sorry. I explained that I was wrong for telling the story and I was wrong for disrespecting her, embarrassing her, and not keeping my promise. However, I understood that my verbal apology meant very little without a change in my behavior. I became determined to rebuild the trust that was broken. And I made it a priority to show Anne respect by honoring her—my goal was to return to being a 'man of my word.'

"Over the next few months I went to a counselor, desiring to understand why I was placing what I wanted over what I promised Anne. At home I looked for every opportunity to model respect to Anne by keeping my word. Through counsel and healing, I began to understand some of my insecurities and family-of-origin propensities—in this specific instance, wanting to be the life of the party.

"A main focus for me was to make certain that my yes was yes and my no was no. Slowly, over time, trust was restored. Looking back, one piece of gold I came away with was understanding that as much as Anne enjoyed when I showed her love, I also needed to make it a top priority to show her respect."

Joe asked her, "Anne, can you give me an example of love and respect from your perspective?"

Anne shared, "Early in our marriage, I became aware of my need to make some changes in my communication style. God began showing me how my words to Tim were often unloving and disrespectful. The problem wasn't so much what I said to Tim but the way I said it.

"While raising our family, we always made it a priority to go out twice a month on a date to spend some time away from the kids and focus on the 'we' of our marriage. Since I'm a conflict avoider by nature, it's easy for me to dismiss potentially difficult conversations that may turn into arguments. But we both agreed to stay current with any conflict so that things didn't pile up.

"I remember one particular date night when I needed to talk with Tim about some marriage concerns, but because of the way Tim is wired, I wanted to do it while showing him love and respect. I set the atmosphere by getting a babysitter and making reservations at one of his favorite restaurants. We enjoyed our meal together while I waited for the right time to address my concern. Sensing that I had something on my heart, Tim said, 'Is everything okay? What's up?'

"'Well,' I told him, 'I did want to talk to you about some things. But before I do, I want to apologize.' Tim looked surprised, obviously wondering what was coming next.

"I continued, 'Lately I've become more aware of my communication style. I've noticed there are times when I'm talking that you seem to shut down. It's usually because I'm being overly dramatic, thinking you'll be more apt to listen. So I tend to make generalizations and exaggerate your flaws. I've realized that at times I sound more like your parent instead of your wife. I just want to tell you that I'm sorry for being unloving and disrespectful to you. Even though that's not my intention, I know it can come across that way. Tim, I respect you more than anyone else I know, and I really want to be your encourager. I want you to know that I'm becoming more aware of how I communicate, and I'm working on showing you more respect in loving ways. I'm sorry; I was wrong—will you forgive me?'

"I don't think Tim was expecting the conversation to go this way. My apology seemed to open his heart. He dropped his defenses and was hanging on my every word. After a long pause, he responded, 'Well, I'm not sure what to say … but thank you. We have had some pretty tough conversations lately. I know you love me, and your apology means a lot. It's not just you; I need to work on things too. For example, I need to become a better listener. Is there anything else you want to talk about?'

"I reached for the pepper shaker and sprinkled a few grains of black pepper on the center of the white linen tablecloth. He smiled and nodded, a little suspicious of my next move.

"Then I said, 'I want to talk to you about a few things that are bothering me. But they are very, very small. In fact, the only reason I'm bringing them up is because I don't want to be a conflict avoider. So this is the new-and-improved version of me. I want to find ways to communicate in love and with respect so that my delivery doesn't detract from what I'm trying to say.'

"After pausing to make sure Tim was following me, I continued with an illustration. 'This white tablecloth represents our life together. These few flecks of black pepper represent the size of the things I want to talk to you about. In fact, they seem so small compared to all the things you are doing right.

"Tim started laughing and said, 'Okay, that was a great start. Now, what did I do?' We both laughed. That evening we were able to work through some potentially explosive topics because our defenses were down and our hearts were open. It wasn't my words as much as the respectful attitude I conveyed to Tim that allowed us to communicate more effectively. The difference in Tim's response was amazing. Looking back, I see that beginning with encouragement—focusing on what Tim was doing right—and meeting Tim's desire for love and respect became the keys that opened his heart and spirit.

"Joe, love and respect are not based on gender. During the love-and-respect section of our REAL LIFE Marriage Advance, we challenge wives to ask their husbands, 'Do you feel loved and respected by me?' We challenge husbands to ask their wives, 'Do you feel loved and respected by me?' A husband or wife giving his or her spouse an opportunity to share his or her heart is an invitation to advance in intimacy.

"God's original design for marital oneness includes intimacy and co-leadership. Men and women who are both made in the image of God—*imago Dei*. Within a plurality of persons—male and female—a couple is invited to **reflect** and **reveal** the diversity within the plurality of the Godhead."

"But how does that play out in real life?" Joe asked.

Anne said, "We have found that our culture, for the most part, understands the concept of unconditional love. However, husbands and wives tend to make respect contingent on a person's behavior. Spouses believe their husband or wife must earn respect, and they withhold it until their spouse behaves in the specific ways they deem acceptable."

Joe asked, "Are you saying I am supposed to love and respect my wife—no matter what?"

"Joe, that's a good question. It's important to clarify: we are not saying someone is commanded to love and respect his or her spouse's poor behavior. For example, a wife may not love and respect the behavior of a husband who continually acts out in narcissistic ways. But she can still treat him with love and respect. Likewise, a husband is not commanded to love and respect the behavior of a wife who makes unwise, self-centered decisions. But he can still treat her with love and respect. Our experience is that whether a spouse is treasured and honored more through love or respect—no matter how long a couple has been married—encouragement, affirmation, and presupposing the best never get old."

Joe said, "Okay, I'm beginning to see that love and respect are not gender specific. But help me understand, aren't husbands and wives supposed to live out certain predetermined roles?"

Roles

"Joe, similar to love and respect, roles are not gender exclusive. We believe the primary role for every man and woman is to live out the Great Commandment—love. In marriage, we encourage both husbands and wives to focus on the role of being a servant. They are to humbly walk together as co-leaders and reciprocal servants and function in the gifts God has given each of them, doing what works best in their marriage; of course this is different for different couples. Together they celebrate unity and diversity, rather than trying to force each other into predetermined roles based on gender."

Joe asked, "But as the husband, aren't I responsible to man up, to be a man's man and step into the role of being the head and the leader?"

"Joe, can I ask, is leadership a strong gift God has given you? Because we know husbands with strong gifts of leadership. But often when they exercise those gifts, they fail to include their wives. The result is that the benefits and blessings in co-leadership get compromised. We meet other husbands who do not have strong leadership gifts. They can get easily discouraged when they fail to meet traditional religious gender expectations. In fact, sometimes it's the wife who doesn't seem satisfied with what she perceives as her husband's, to use your terms, lack of 'manning up' and being a 'man's man.' Many church leaders default to telling husbands they do not lead right, pray enough, parent the kids well, lead in devotions enough, manage the finances effectively, or provide the spiritual cover they are responsible to provide over their wives.

"Our experience is many husbands get frustrated and desert—they may check out emotionally, physically, spiritually—and others just give up. Regrettably, some husbands get so discouraged, they reach the conclusion that *I'll never be the spiritual leader my wife wants and church leaders say I'm supposed to be, so why bother*? And they invest their time and energy in other interests."

Joe asked, "Can you give me an example of a marriage where the wife has the strong leadership gifts?"

I told him, "God has given a good friend of ours amazing helps and service gifts, and his wife has been blessed with amazing leadership gifts. He has told us on a number of occasions that at home things work smoothly. But in the church he experiences shame as leaders convey—subtly and not so subtly—that he 'needs to man up, become a man's man, and step into his God-ordained role as the spiritual leader in his marriage.' He also describes how church leaders convey—subtly and not so subtly—to him and to his leadership-gifted wife that 'she is coming on too strong and needs to tone it down a bit.'"

Being a "Man's Man"

Joe interjected, "But to be totally honest, one of my life goals is to be known as a man's man."

"Joe," I said, "after growing up in a family with five males, including a dad who was a decorated World War II soldier and Golden Gloves boxing champion; after retiring as a deputy fire chief from a twenty-plus-year career in the fire service with one hundred and fifty men (no women were firefighters at that time); and after a lifetime in local churches, I think I understand your take on being a man's man. However, at this season in my life, I believe the typical man's-man portrayal—one I've found in many churches and men's ministries—is more often than not a mixed bag."

"A mixed bag in what ways?"

"The 'man up, man's man' mantra often includes high machismo—defined as 'an exaggerated sense or display of masculinity, emphasizing characteristics that are conventionally regarded as male, usually physical strength and courage, aggressiveness, and lack of emotional response.'[19] Add to this a measure of male insecurity, centuries of misogyny, patriarchy, and hierarchy, as well as an overall misunderstanding of true biblical manhood, and this can become a male-gender recipe for disaster—and sadly, women (especially wives) are often the first to be impacted by the negative fallout. In addition, there are other factors, including culture, environment, and season of history that play into man's-man views and perceptions."

Joe asked, "How do culture and history play into male roles?"

"For example, a man's man in the Western United States a century ago was the man who rode a horse all day, handled guns well, had sex with lots of women, and smoked and drank lots of whiskey. A man's man in the sports world is typically the man who runs the fastest, jumps the highest, is the strongest and toughest. And don't even get me started about how Hollywood portrays a man's man. In the mid-1970s when I began my fire-department career (before we used self-contained breathing apparatuses) the man's man was the fireman who could inhale the most smoke.

Called a 'leather lunger' he was the man's man everyone looked up to. Sadly, most leather lungers died early from lung cancer."

Joe said, "I hear what you're saying, but it sounds like you are implying there's something wrong with wanting to be a man's man—is that what you are saying?"

"Joe, for me personally, instead of being known as a man's man in the ways it's typically described in our culture, churches, and men's ministries, I would prefer to be known as a man who loved God with all his heart, soul, mind, and strength. My desire is to be known as a one-woman man who passionately loved his bride well for his entire lifetime. I'd like to be known as a man who captured the hearts of his wife, kids, spiritual kids, grandkids—a man who loved God, was a faithful spouse, a great dad and granddad. And I'd like to be known as a man who came to crossroads in his life and chose the more difficult path. A warrior-poet friend of mine puts it this way:

> Be careful what you wish for.
> If you wish to be a man's man
> you might find yourself at the end
> a hard-pressed man who missed
> the daily frailties that soften you
> allowing you to close your eyes
> and rest in peace. Perhaps the
> grander wish is to be a woman's man
> or a child's man or a dog's man.
> Those are the men missed when
> they are finally gone.[20]

Joe said, "Tim—okay, I hear what you're saying, but God is a God of order. You gotta understand there are specific roles that men and women must fit into."

"Joe, my encouragement to you—to *both* husbands and wives—is to grow in your true identity. Explore the good, not-so-good, and negative aspects in your family of origin. Invest in understanding and living out how God has uniquely created and gifted *you*. Know your strengths and weaknesses, understand your temperament, love language, style of relating, and spiritual gifts. Invest in getting healing from life's hurts that every person experiences. Then together with your wife, embrace and celebrate your uniqueness and diversity. As equals and as co-leaders, **I.O.T.L.** *(inquire of the Lord)* and prayerfully discern how God can best use you *both*—your marriage and story—to bring Him glory and advance His kingdom."

"Do you know a Bible passage that addresses that type of gender equality?" Joe asked.

"One passage is in Galatians. It reads: 'So in Christ Jesus you are *all* children of God through faith, for *all* of you who were baptized into Christ have clothed yourselves with Christ. There is neither Jew nor Gentile, neither slave nor free, nor is there male and female, for you are *all* one in Christ Jesus.'[21]

"Joe, it's important to note, when that Galatians passage was written, Jewish men regularly prayed: 'Thank You, God, that I am *not* a Gentile, a slave, *or a female.*' When we review the ways Gentiles, slaves, and women were treated at that time in history, we see that this passage leveled the playing field—making this teaching revolutionary. Unfortunately, this is not a popular passage male church leaders preach about."

Joe said, "Throughout my entire life—in Sunday school, at youth group, and in churches—I've been told that as the man I am the leader and that when I got married I would have authority over my wife."

"Joe, yes, some do believe that man was created with a measure of intrinsic authority and a functional leadership role based on gender. However, we don't see any evidence of these in the beginning before sin entered the marriage story. Furthermore, how about we review God engaging with the man and woman after sin?"

"Sounds good," Joe agreed.

"Joe, after the man and woman sinned, God confronted them. Notice He specifically placed enmity—defined as mutual hatred and ill will—between the woman and the serpent. Stop and think about this: if the man was designed to be the leader and spiritual cover, wouldn't it make sense for God to place enmity between the *man* and the serpent—not between the *woman* and the serpent?"

"I've never heard that gender perspective," Joe said, "or realized the significance of God placing enmity between the serpent and the *woman*."

"You know, Joe, we wonder—*what if many church and cultural gender roles are not based on God's original design for maleness and femaleness?* For example, what if God's description of the first woman (*ezer*)—warrior, strength, savior, power, protector—was embraced? With that *ezer* interpretation, every woman would be encouraged to step into her true identity and the gifts and callings God has given her.

"Joe, it's not my desire to sound disparaging, but frankly I get tired of male religious leaders claiming that the real key to kingdom-of-God advancement is for husbands to step up, man up, and become a man's man. Certainly husbands stepping into their true identities and engaging more in marriage and relationships will bring a measure of kingdom-of-God advancement. However, in my opinion, the kingdom of God will advance more successfully if husbands focus on their true identities—how God uniquely wired and gifted them—and then focus on celebrating and embracing the intrinsic God-given strengths in their wives as they encourage them to step into their pre-fall *ezer* calling. Unfortunately, when it comes to many local church and parachurch ministries, the Enemy has in effect cunningly neutralized half the church and half of marriages; the powerhouse in husband-wife co-leadership is compromised.

"Joe, all that is to say, if the husband is in fact created to be God's designated leader, the go-to person in marriage who is in charge because he has some unique God-given intrinsic male leadership DNA; and if wives are lacking this leadership DNA and are created to be subordinate to their husbands' superior leadership gifts and skills, why do we have no record of women ever betraying or denying Jesus—only men?

"Dr. Mimi Haddad, president of Christians for Biblical Equality, has dedicated her life to championing gender equality. She wrote:

> Scripture boldly compares the failures of the twelve to the courageous faith of women. The twelve grasp for power; they want to sit at Christ's right and left hand (Mark 10:37); they forbid even children to approach Jesus (Mark 10:13); they are outraged and humiliated when Christ speaks with women openly (John 4:27); and one even betrays Christ. When He is arrested and crucified, the twelve disperse, one denies Christ openly, and others hole up behind locked doors.

Yet, the women remain brave-hearted and faithful throughout. They understand that Christ's mission will end on the cross, and they tenderly prepare his body for death. They remain with Christ during his crucifixion, and wrap his body in grave clothes. Outside the tomb, they wait faithfully—a vigilance that Christ rewards. A woman—Mary—is the first to meet the risen Lord. Christ tells her to go to his disciples with the good news! Do they believe her? Did they believe Christ? Even as Jesus appears to them, Thomas asks to touch his wounds just to be sure it *is* Christ."[22]

"Then how do you walk out roles in your marriage?" Joe asked.

Functions

"Joe, instead of focusing on roles, which in our experience can lead to all sorts of misunderstanding and unrighteous judgments, we focus more on functions. There are specific circumstances—for example the counseling aspect of REAL LIFE ministries—in which Anne functions more in a leadership capacity, so she leads. And there are specific circumstances—for example when we lead REAL LIFE marriage gatherings—in which I function more in a leadership capacity, then I will lead. Our desire is to maximize the gifts God has given *both* of us. For example, God has given Anne amazing wisdom, discernment, counseling, and teaching gifts, and He has given me a double portion of encouragement, leadership, prayer, and faith gifts. In our marriage we try to make the best use of *all* our gifts."

Joe asked, "Okay, but how do you do that?"

"Practically we make it a top marriage priority to utilize the **Traffic Light Principle**: first we **I.O.T.L.** *(inquire of the Lord)*; we implement co-leadership; and we make decisions only when we *both* have green lights. We function best in this way: not acting based on who is male, who is female, or who has a specific predetermined role. Our focus is on loving and serving God and each other. Looking back over decades of marriage, we believe co-leading in unity and not focusing on roles has provided us with immeasurable power and protection."

Joe interjected, "But Tim, who is the leader in your marriage?"

"Joe, it's Jesus. We sincerely believe the best leaders are the best followers. Jesus, the quintessential servant-leader, said, 'Follow Me.'[23] As we've said, our top priority is focusing on following Jesus and then co-leading—*together*—"

Joe interrupted. "But the fact is Jesus came to earth as a *man*—not as a *woman*."

"Joe, the Bible states emphatically that God is not a man.[24] God essence transcends sexuality and gender. Making God into a 'male' borders on idolatry—creating a false God. Remember, God's Trinitarian nature is a mystery that includes both masculine and feminine characteristics. For example, there are texts that focus on the more stereotypical masculine characteristics of God: 'The LORD is a warrior; the LORD is His Name.'[25] And there are texts that focus on the more stereotypical feminine-like comforting and merciful characteristics of God: 'Blessed be the God and Father of our Lord Jesus Christ, the Father of mercies and God of all comfort; who comforts us in our affliction so that we may be able to comfort those who are in any affliction with which we ourselves are comforted by God.'[26] And the apostle Paul—a true man's man—wrote to the church in

Thessalonica, saying, 'We proved to be gentle among you, as a nursing mother tenderly cares for her own children. Having thus a fond affection for you....'"[27]

I continued, "Look at the life of Jesus: He modeled a full range of feelings and life experiences. Jesus lived adventures—rebuking storms, healing people, bringing dead people back to life. And Jesus engaged in battles—after His baptism the Holy Spirit led Jesus into the wilderness for a power encounter with Satan. Throughout His life Jesus regularly engaged with demons and rebuked religious and political leaders."

Joe responded, "That's right, Jesus was a man's man!"

I replied, "Joe, it's important to remember that Jesus also experienced feelings of sadness, anger, fear, happiness, excitement, and tenderness. Jesus modeled love, humility, gentleness, and compassion. He treated women with unheard-of honor and respect; He embraced children, spoke lovingly to outcasts, washed men's feet, and openly wept. All that is to say, if Jesus were to describe Himself, what words do you think He would use?"

Joe said, "I'm not sure. Probably *warrior, strength, savior, power, protector* ..."

I told him, "I agree with all your terms to describe Jesus. But you know what, Joe? The words you just used to describe Jesus are strikingly similar to the meaning of God's description of the first *woman*: *ezer*, which means 'warrior, strength, savior, power, protector—'"

Joe interrupted. "Frankly, I'm not all that interested in the precise meaning of *ezer*. Tim, please answer this question—how did Jesus describe

Himself? As the quintessential example of a man's man, what words did He use?"

"Jesus described Himself only one time in the Bible, in Matthew 11:29. He said, 'I am *gentle and humble in heart.*' Joe, are *gentleness* and *humility* words you would use to describe a quintessential man's man?"

"No—probably not, but there are so many popular messages that focus on gender and roles."

"Joe, be discerning in regards to popular messages that absolutize gender and roles. For example, Jesus never said that respect was the key to His personal fulfillment, longings, or desires. And throughout His life He was both tough and tender—a warrior and a lover—depending on the circumstances. But, thinking back to the beginning of our conversation, when Jesus described Himself as *gentle and humble in heart*, Joe—aren't those the exact words you used to describe a *woman*?"

Joe replied, "Yes, I guess I did. But men and women are so different."

"That's correct, but remember, *different is good*! And differences between husbands and wives vary from individual to individual and from couple to couple. Differences, variety, and diversity should be celebrated and never used to restrict or control. In marriage, the key is for husbands and wives—as co-leaders—to focus on love. Together **reflecting** and **revealing** the heart of God to their spouse, living out *unity trumps disunity*, living in the Larger Story, and declaring through their attitude and behavior that *marriage is not about me.*"

Joe said, "Tim, I appreciate your and Anne's take on love, respect, roles, and gender equality—I truly do. But, bottom line for me—the way I've been taught in churches my entire life—in marriage the husband is the person who wears the pants."

"Joe, after being married almost four decades, we find our marriage works best—and is by far the most fun—when neither of us wears any pants!"

CHAPTER 11

CO-LEADERSHIP IS LIBERATING FOR EVERYONE

Life Is Lived in a Story

tim+anne

At a marriage gathering, a woman we will refer to as Leah and her husband, Matt, stayed afterward to talk with us. Leah was very articulate, and shortly into our conversation it became obvious to us that she had strong leadership gifts.

Anne asked, "Leah, I'm wondering, as a young wife and mom, how do you feel about our pre-fall teaching regarding God's original marriage design, specifically in the ways we encourage husbands and wives to walk out co-leadership together in mutual equality and mutual authority?"

Leah responded, "I've faithfully attended church my entire life. As I look back, even before Matt and I got married, I was told by religious leaders that if I ever married, my husband would become my spiritual leader and my spiritual cover because he would be the head who has authority over me. But now I am excited about walking out co-leadership in our marriage."

"How do you feel about the traditional-hierarchical-complementarian marriage perspectives?" Anne asked.

"Gosh—that's a good question. I know both my and Matt's grandparents lived out the traditional-hierarchical marriage view, and both our parents refer to their marriage view as complementarian. I haven't totally processed this, but it almost feels that in the traditional-hierarchical-complementarian marriage views I don't have to or shouldn't step into what I sense is my true identity in Christ.

"What do you mean by your true identity?" Anne asked.

Leah replied, "As I study the traditional-hierarchical-complementarian marriage views, they restrict my ability to fully reflect and reveal my gifts and callings as a woman made in the image of God. For example, if Matt is my spiritual leader and spiritual cover who has authority over me, then as we walk that out I can see how I might be limited in stepping into all God has created and gifted me to be. This could open the door for me as a wife to develop an unhealthy dependency, potential codependency, on Matt as he takes on the role of spiritual leader and mediator between me and God."

"Leah, we're not sure what you mean; help us understand."

"Well, if Matt does have some form of spiritual authority over me, then where does Jesus fit in for me as a wife? In the Bible Jesus declared, 'All authority in heaven and on earth has been given to me.'[1] The apostle Paul wrote, 'For there is one God and one mediator between God and humankind' and that is Jesus Christ.[2] Isn't Jesus my authority, my leader, mediator, and spiritual cover?"

Leah continued, "The more I understand and live out my true identity in Christ, I realize that I don't long for a leader or spiritual cover as much as I long for a partner to co-lead together with. In church I've been taught that the male rulership and traditional-hierarchical-complementarian marriage views include a functional hierarchy where I defer to Matt in making decisions because he is my leader and he has spiritual authority over me. But it seems that contradicts the mutual authority clearly commanded to both the husband and wife in 1 Corinthians 7. To me the male rulership and traditional-hierarchical-complementarian marriage views, where Matt is functionally first and I am second, do not align with God's original marriage design of togetherness in co-leadership."

"Leah, please tell us more about your understanding of co-leadership."

"I guess when I read about God's original marriage design before sin entered the marriage story, I see God creating a wife—an *ezer*—to rescue man from his 'not good' condition of aloneness. Before sin, woman was never designed to hold back or suppress who she was created to be. God created *both* the man and woman to **reflect** and **reveal** His image, plurality, and goodness. And God commanded *both* the man and woman to carry out the dominion and procreation mandates, co-leading together and celebrating being naked and not ashamed."

"Matt, how do you feel about everything Leah is saying?" we asked.

Matt said, "First, let me say we both continue to study the Genesis and New Testament marriage passages. As far as our marriage, God has given Leah a capital-L leadership gift. She is also an amazing teacher. Of course Leah is a great wife and mom, but she also gets over-the-top evaluations at work. Heck, she regularly leads mission trips overseas that consist of both women and men. After every trip they affirm Leah's leadership and teaching gifts. I often say to my friends that I married an amazing, uniquely gifted woman."

Matt continued, "From my perspective, why would I not want Leah to bring *all* the gifts God has given her to our marriage? Personally, I don't see benefits in a marital hierarchy, where I have some perceived authority over Leah. For me, co-leading encourages interdependence instead of independence or unhealthy co-dependency. I believe God invites Leah and me as equals—as co-leaders and co-laborers together for Christ—to become one in spirit, soul, and body. The bottom line in our marriage is we believe God is the best cover-leader-head-authority over *both* of us."

Leah added, "The interesting part in our story is Matt is an amazing leader too. Ever since he played sports as a little boy he was always selected as team captain by his peers. And after he gave his heart and life to Jesus, his leadership gifts increased exponentially. In fact, every time we take spiritual-gift assessments, we both rate extremely high on leadership."

We replied, "It's so great that you know your spiritual gifts—that helps you to function as the part of the church body God has uniquely gifted you to be."

Leah responded, "Thanks. But it's like I am encouraged, even rewarded when I step into the gifts and calling God has given me—everywhere except in the church. But when I am around religious leaders and the topic turns to marriage, I hear over and over that as my husband, Matt is my spiritual leader and spiritual cover who has authority over me. In all honesty, there are times at church when I feel as if some religious leaders would prefer me not to use all the gifts the Holy Spirit has given me. I believe most church leaders are doing their best, but at times they convey to me that I should put the gifts God has given me in a box and use them only in predetermined ways."

"In what ways?" we asked.

"Well, if my gifts were encouragement, mercy, helps, or hospitality, these gifts would be celebrated by church leaders. But my gifts of leadership and teaching seem to be restricted by many leaders just because I am a woman. You know, I never asked to be a leader and teacher; these are gifts that blossomed after I gave my heart and life to Jesus. When I review my life with Matt and most of our friends, I feel celebrated and encouraged to be all God created me to be. And in my career, both men and women encourage me and cheer me on to use all my gifts. But at church I often feel my leadership and teaching gifts are devalued."

We told her, "We hear you, and we believe most male church leaders are good men who are trying to accurately interpret and live out marriage and gender passages as best they can."

Matt asked, "Why do you think the church treats women so differently from the workplace?"

"Matt, that's a good question. Remember, this is not a clear-cut case of one view or interpretation verses another. When it comes to gender, there are deeper aspects involved. For centuries in society and churches there has been a culture of male rulership, misogyny, hierarchy, discrimination, and untold abuses toward women. And never forget there is a spiritual component in play. There is an Enemy who hates marriage and who understands the potential marriage has to advance the kingdom of God. That is why the Enemy tries to distort what true equality and togetherness in co-leadership looks like."

Leah interjected, "You know, there are times I struggle with some of my girlfriends who are pro-complementarian marriage."

"In what ways?" we asked.

"One of my girlfriends believes her husband is her leader and spiritual cover. When I describe the ways Matt and I live out co-leadership, she gets angry and insists that her way is the right way, the only way to biblically live out marriage. Another older woman, an elder's wife, attended our women's small group and asked me to explain co-leadership."

"How did you respond?" Anne asked.

"I explained to the elder's wife and to the girls in our group that Matt and I were still learning, and I emphasized that our marriage view was not a salvation issue or an absolute—but a preference. Then I opened the Bible to Genesis and shared about God's original design of co-leadership in mutual equality and mutual authority before sin entered the story."

"And how'd that go?" Anne asked.

"Not very well. The elder's wife appeared to get upset; she opened her Bible and quoted a few New Testament passages. Then, in front of everyone, she said that in her opinion I did not truly understand a biblical marriage or a wife's role. She said that Matt was not leading as a husband is supposed to, and if my primary marriage focus was on equality and co-leadership instead of submission, then in her opinion I was being rebellious."

Anne said, "Leah, we're so sorry you had to endure spiritual malpractice from that elder's wife. How did you feel when you were treated so disrespectfully?"

"I guess at first I felt shame—frankly, I was shocked that she came on so strong, especially in front of our entire Bible study. I also felt angry because I felt violated and discounted. But, as I reviewed the elder's wife confronting me, of course her words really hurt. But looking back, it seemed that she appeared to be more scared than angry toward me."

"Scared?" we asked.

"Yes. I'm not sure, but it was as if she had no reasonable response to what I described about marriage. When I asked her specifically about mutual authority and co-leadership, she acted as if she had never even heard of that marriage view. That's where I think she may have been more scared than angry. As I reviewed the meeting, I realized there was no back-and-forth interaction. This woman just opened her Bible and began quoting Scripture. I guess overall our exchange felt kind of awkward and disappointing to me."

Anne asked, "I'm wondering, in addition to feeling shame and anger, did you feel anything else?"

"Anne, not in the moment of the exchange, but as I continue to process all that occurred, I guess both Matt and I feel sad that they're missing out. For us, co-leading in marriage maximizes how God uniquely creates and gifts both a husband and wife. I feel sad when I observe how many of my friends' gifts are controlled and restricted in marriage and in the church world—what a loss. I also feel sad when I think about all the untapped kingdom-advancing potential within God's original design of together-ness in co-leadership."

"Leah, our experience is that often, more religious-oriented people strug-gle with co-leadership the most."

"Why do you think that is?" Matt asked.

"Matt, one thing we've noticed is that when women who were raised in traditional churches begin to explore co-leadership and implement the **Traffic Light Principle**, many of them struggle. This is understandable because most churches and seminaries teach traditional-hierarchical-complementarian marriage views in which the husband is the wife's authority, leader, and spiritual cover. This plays out as the husband hav-ing authority to make final decisions, because in these marriage views, gender trumps over mutual submission,[3] mutual authority,[4] and recipro-cal servanthood.[5] When marital chaos surfaces, wives are reminded—at times reprimanded—that the husband is God's designated authority and that one of a wife's primary roles is to submit to her husband. Sadly, in many churches, the culture of love, unity, community, and oneness that Jesus brought with Him has been replaced with a culture of hierarchy, male leadership, and female subordination."

Leah asked, "Do you have any suggestions for how I can respond in loving ways to my girlfriends when I talk about co-leadership?"

"Leah, we encourage you to first **I.O.T.L.** *(inquire of the Lord)*. He has wisdom and resources beyond our understanding. Continue studying marriage in the beginning. Then work on humbly and passionately living in the Larger Story as you model co-leadership with Matt. Lastly, encourage your girlfriends to pray, study, and process with their husbands God's original marriage design."

Leah replied, "What about relating to my traditional-hierarchical-complementarian and more religious-orientated girlfriends and church leaders?"

"Be forewarned that women who are set in traditional-hierarchical-complementarian marriage views often bristle at the possibility of co-leading with their husband. Most of these women have lived their entire married lives being told that their husband is their authority—their leader and spiritual cover—and they have grown comfortable submitting and leaving the responsibility for final decision making up to him. Now, if it's working for them and the husband and wife are in agreement, that's fine.

"But, after working with couples for decades, we've come to a number of hypotheses."

"What hypotheses have you arrived at?" Leah asked.

Tim responded, "Leah, this may be a long shot, but could wives who have an inordinate desire for their husbands to lead, be their spiritual cover, and have the final say in the decision-making process ... might they be living out a marriage view that is connected to the consequences of the fall, when God said to the woman, 'Your desire will be for your husband, and he shall rule over you'?[6] We meet many women who look to their husbands, rather than to God, to meet their needs for security, leadership, and direction. Makes us wonder: *could this be an indication a wife might be living under the consequences of the fall—instead of living out God's original marriage design of co-leadership, mutual equality, and mutual authority?*

"Leah, taking this a bit deeper: regarding wives who prefer a marriage view that includes the husband having a primary leadership role and functional authority—okay, this may be another long shot, but we wonder ... *is it possible these wives might be abdicating their God given image bearer identity and responsibility to step into the mutual authority and co-leadership God created them to live out?* Remember, *in the beginning* God gave both the husband and the wife the procreation mandate and rulership (dominion) mandate."

Leah said, "Tim, I'm pretty sure none of my more religious-oriented, complementarian marriage-view girl friends have ever connected their view of the husband being their leader and spiritual cover as a possible consequence of the fall, or as abdicating their responsibility to co-lead together with their husband."

"Leah, in addition to observing wives who focus on the husband being the leader and spiritual cover and who make a wife's submission—instead of mutual submission—the pearl of great price in marriage, we have noticed another aspect in some marriages. This involves a marriage/church culture with a spiritually gifted female leader who religiously tries to fit into traditional-hierarchical-complementarian marriage/church views. Our experience is that this situation opens the door to frustration and often leads a woman to be led by the Enemy into passive-aggressive behavior. We've met godly women who are blessed with amazing gifts. They have so much potential to co-lead in marriage, build up the church, and advance God's kingdom. Unfortunately, our sense is they are being neutralized in the full use of the gifts God has given them because of the ways that male rulership and traditional-hierarchical-complementarian marriage/church views are taught and walked out."

Matt asked; "have you developed any hypotheses for husbands?"

Tim replied, "yes, and once again this may be another long shot, but a husband who has an inordinate desire for having authority, being the leader, spiritual cover, and having the final say ... might he be living out a marriage view that is connected to the consequences of the fall as described at the end of Genesis 3:16 where God said to the woman; "And he shall rule over you.

"We meet many traditional-hierarchical-complementarian husbands who, after hearing our co-leadership marriage message, tell us it stirs something in their hearts that resonates with the mutual equality and mutual authority God originally designed for marriage. Makes us wonder: *could this be an indication that many male rulership and traditional-hierarchical-complementarian husbands might be living under the consequences of the fall—instead of living out God's original co-leadership marriage design?*

"Tim, those hypotheses are really interesting, but help us understand—since different marriage views are preferences and not absolutes, aren't most couples excited to give co-leadership a try?" Matt asked.

MANY HUSBANDS ENJOY HAVING THE FINAL SAY

Tim said, "That's a great question, Matt. When I talk privately with men at our Advances, I ask them how they feel about our co-leadership marriage challenge. Most younger men are overwhelmingly positive and eager to give co-leadership a try. However, more religiously trained men will often try to deflect my question. If I push back and press them, they say, 'Tim, the bottom line for me is I guess I like my theology and my interpretation of Bible passages that give me authority in my marriage. Truth be told, I enjoy having the final say.'

"Matt and Leah, we sincerely believe a husband's unspoken response—*I like having the final say*—lies at the heart of much of the resistance to returning to God's original co-leadership marriage principles."

"Wow. That's pretty telling, isn't it?" Leah said.

"Leah, in addition to observing that many men want the final say, throughout the years we've developed a more subjective observation about marriage. We believe in the old adage 'The eyes are the window to the soul' as well as another familiar slogan: 'A wife's face is her husband's résumé.' And after looking directly into the eyes of countless wives who live in traditional-hierarchical-complementarian marriages—and after hearing their stories—we sense in many of them a lack of joy, passion, and purpose, as well as hearts that are not fully alive.

"We believe marriages will not maximize their kingdom-advancing potential as long as husbands take the position that they are the leader, the spiritual cover, and the head defined as having authority over their wives. We've found that many husbands view marriage and the decision-making process as if they have a gender trump card in their back pocket. Unless a decision involves something illegal or immoral, the husband can trump his wife and have the final say. And our experience is, more often than not, that many husbands who like having the final say have issues related to insecurity, fear, and control."

Matt asked, "Can you share what you've learned as you've traveled in regard to men's responses to different marriage views?"

Tim said, "Matt, here's a quick overview. We've seen men falling into a number of different groups. In group one, husbands prefer what we call the male rulership, the traditional, or the hierarchical marriage view. A man in this group is convinced that he is God's designated leader and his wife's spiritual cover and that as head he has authority and the final say in making decisions. In male rulership and traditional-hierarchical marriage views, *gender trumps*.

"Group two includes husbands who like to refer to themselves as complementarians—the wife complements the husband and the husband complements the wife. In this marriage view, husbands make an extra effort to include their wives in making decisions. But, when pressed about who has authority, they define head as the husband having authority and, if necessary, the final say in making decisions—similar to male rulership and traditional-hierarchical marriage views. In the complementarian marriage view, *gender trumps*.

"Group three includes husbands who prefer what we call the egalitarian marriage view. Husbands and wives embrace co-leadership in mutual equality and mutual authority. Egalitarians believe in mutual submission. Head is defined as source or servant-provider, and there is no hierarchy or forced female subordination. The egalitarian decision-making process includes a number of components. Decisions are based on gifts, not gender, and couples pre-agree on what they will do if they reach an impasse. For example, if a decision affects the wife more than the husband, she has authority to make the call. In the egalitarian marriage view, *process trumps*.

"The men in group four prefer God's original marriage design. This involves co-leadership in mutual equality and mutual authority where there is not a focus on headship, hierarchy, male authority, or female subordination. Unlike in other marriage views, in this marriage design neither gender nor process trumps. In the co-leadership marriage model, first the husband and wife **I.O.T.L**. If they do not *both* have green lights from God, they do not pull the trigger on decisions. In God's original co-leadership marriage design, *Unity Triumphs*."

Matt replied; "Thanks, that helps. Tim, can I ask, how do you feel about the ongoing conversation surrounding marriage and gender equality?"

"Matt, apart from so much unloving vitriol and unkind dialogue, my humble opinion is most church leaders are good men who are following generations of patriarchy and hierarchy. My personal experience is that in many churches it's the men doing the leading, teaching, and preaching, and unfortunately—all too often—very little listening."

Leah asked; "Tim, if you were given the opportunity, what might you say to women?"

"Gosh, Leah that's a great question. First, I would **I.O.T.L.** My sense is God would invite me to ask women for forgiveness. I would say that as a man, husband, ordained minister and male church leader, on behalf of myself and countless men-husbands-ministers and male church leaders who have been unkind, unfair, and discounting....I am so sorry. I would look them in the eyes and describe how my heart is grieved when I think about all that marriages and churches are missing out on because of the ways wives and women are restricted from using all the gifts the Holy Spirit has given them. Women who could add so much to marriage-family life, church life, and to advancing the kingdom of God.

Leah responded; "Tim, first, as a woman your apology touched something in my heart, thank you. Second, looking ahead, what do you and Anne sense as far as next steps surrounding our culture, marriage, and male and female relationships?"

"Leah, as anne+i look at our culture, as we **I.O.T.L,** we continue to pray for a day when the kindness of God will lead to repentance.[7] We envision the Holy Spirit, who is truth, guiding men and women into all truth.[8] Through repentance and humility our sense is God is going to invite humble men-husbands-ministers-and male church leaders throughout the world to individually and corporately apologize, and to ask for forgiveness from wives and women who have not been nourished, cherished, and celebrated as equals—and co-leaders."

CHANGE INVOLVES RISK—AND INCLUDES GETTING MESSY

Matt asked, "Tim, I know that we've covered a lot, but before we move on, do you think church leaders will embrace your and Anne's co-leadership marriage message?"

"We sure hope so, but sad to say, while many church leaders talk about marriage and gender equality, when you look at church leadership positions, elder/overseer boards, teachers at church conferences, and who is in the pulpits—these positions and ministry opportunities are all overwhelmingly biased toward men."

"What will it take for church leaders to embrace change?"

"Matt, that's a great question. Our experience is that embracing change includes being open to allowing things to get messy. Looking back, we are grateful for our twenty years at Willow Creek Community Church. From the early years, Bill and Lynne Hybels, the elders, and church leaders valued all the gifts the Holy Spirit gave to women. They didn't just talk about letting women lead; they prayerfully and courageously broke down religious and cultural barriers."

"In what ways?" Leah asked.

"They appointed women elders and board directors. They encouraged women to exercise the gifts the Holy Spirit gave them in every church office, role, and function. They provided opportunities for women to teach, preach, and lead ministries. They humbly took a stand for women and gender equality—and at times it got pretty messy, as they received lots of criticism and unrighteous judgment."

"What do you mean change includes things getting messy?" Leah asked.

"Leading a church, living out marriage, parenting children, being in relationships—living life gets messy. For reasons we don't fully understand, church leaders tend to resist hosting and promoting marriage gatherings that focus on co-leadership. Their position is they don't want to deal with the potential mess that encouraging couples to co-lead in mutual equality and mutual authority might create."

Leah asked, "Why do you suppose they respond like that?"

"Leah, that's another great question. Our experience is that many church leaders have no problem opening their churches to financial seminars—even though it gets messy and creates chaos when people seriously explore finances. More charismatic church leaders have no problem opening their churches to prayer, prophetic, and healing gatherings—and this often leads to messes that need to be cleaned up and chaos that needs to be sorted through."

Matt asked, "Can you think of other issues where church leaders have resisted change and things got messy?"

"The church has experienced many adjustments in its theology and teachings. Throughout history we see things miraculously shifting as God intervened. For example, Old Testament biblical patriarchs, New Testament church leaders, and practically all men and women for quite some time believed that slavery was biblically acceptable.[9]

"The history of slavery reveals that church leaders justified their position based on their 'infallible' interpretation of a handful of passages in the word of God, including Colossians 3:23, Colossians 4:1, Ephesians 6:5, and Titus 2:9–10. It's inconceivable to believe from our perspective today, but if a person literally interprets and absolutizes Bible passages that address slavery, it's possible to see how someone could choose to support inequality and slavery. But, thankfully God provided fresh revelation in regard to the despicable and dehumanizing practice of slavery.

"But this makes us wonder: might it be possible that—similar to the season of church history when God provided fresh understanding about the handful of scriptures religious leaders interpreted as supporting inequality and slavery—we are entering a season of church history when God is providing fresh understanding about a handful of scriptures religious leaders interpret as supporting male authority in marriage and in the church? Looking back a hundred and fifty years, courageous church leaders humbly reviewed their fallible interpretations and passionately stood up against slavery—and as you know, in America it got pretty messy as it divided families and became one of the reasons for the Civil War."

Leah asked, "Help us understand—how does the abolition of slavery relate to marriage?"

"We love this quote by Dr. Brené Brown: 'You can choose comfort or you can choose courage, but you can't choose both.'[10] Unfortunately, our experience is that when it comes to giving co-leadership in marriage a try, many church leaders choose comfort over courage."

"Why do you suppose church leaders are resistant to giving co-leadership a try?" Leah asked.

"The vast majority of church leaders are good men who've been trained in traditional marriage views where a husband, as they define head, has authority over his wife. Many church leaders hear about God's original marriage design and tell us that although they agree in many ways with our marriage message, they don't want to introduce co-leadership in marriage to their congregation because they will have to clean up messes that may occur. But our humble sense is that many church leaders' resistance to embrace and promote co-leadership in marriage is not so much about cleaning up potential messes—it's more about maintaining comfort and control."

"But what about the real-life possibility that church leaders will have to clean up messes when co-leadership is taught?" Matt asked.

"First off, dealing with messes is a reality of life and a necessary part of embracing change. However, our experience is that amazing things occur when we encourage people to revisit marriage in the beginning. After we explain the benefits of implementing the co-leadership **Traffic Light Principle**, many couples tell us that we are putting words and biblical texts to what they sense in their hearts is right. For them, rightness includes mutual equality and mutual authority—what we call co-leadership. Couples describe how the heart of co-leadership is based on grace and equality rather than on the law and hierarchy. Furthermore, apart from a small percentage of more highly religious-orientated people and churches, when we teach co-leadership, the messes leaders anticipate rarely surface as they fear."

"Are there certain groups of people who respond positively to co-leadership?" Leah asked.

"Yes! Sharing about marriage with the millennial generation is exciting. They respond to our co-leadership marriage message with courage and passion. And most millennials are not afraid if things get messy—amazingly, many millennials want to embrace the mess.

"Thankfully, in addition to millennials, it's exciting to meet seasoned church and para-church leaders who are willing to reexamine their traditional marriage theology. As they revisit marriage in the beginning they are starting to question some of the marriage absolutes they have been taught."

"That is so exciting" Leah responded.

"Leah, Anne and my sense is God is in the insipient stage of building a co-leadership marriage team of courageous elders, church staff, and lay-leadership women and men who are becoming united in heart about a mission—God and marriage—that matters."

"Leah and I are millennials; why do you think millennials respond so positively to co-leadership?" Matt asked.

"Our sense is that many millennials have lived in families where their parents got divorced, or they had parents who modeled marriage poorly. Millennials tell us that when they look at marriages, they find many couples lacking passion and purpose. They don't see a lot of seasoned married couples together advancing God's kingdom. Millennials have a hunger to understand why God created marriage. And, as they soberly evaluate the current state of marriage in their families of origin and in many communities of faith, they want more."

"What next steps do you sense?" Leah asked.

"Reviewing church history, we believe God is up to something. And after working with couples for decades, we sense God is getting ready to provide fresh revelation about marriage. As millennials, single men and women, seasoned couples, and teachable church and para-church leaders humbly embrace co-leadership in marriage, the walls of functional inequality and hierarchy will be torn down.

"Another positive outcome is that when women (married and single) are embraced and celebrated for being intrinsically and functionally equal—not just with words, but with actions—doors will open for countless women who have been restricted by husbands and church leaders to bring all the gifts the Holy Spirit has given them to marriage and to the church."

"Are there any places where women are embraced and encouraged to use all their gifts?" Leah asked.

"Leah, it's exciting to see God opening up new opportunities for women. For example, women in the marketplace and in many para-church ministries—especially women with strong leadership and teaching gifts—are being treated as equals, encouraged as colleagues, and celebrated as co-leaders in the use of all their gifts. However, even with these advances, it saddens us that many husbands and local church leaders continue to restrict and limit women."

Leah replied, "saddens you, in what ways?"

"It saddens us that many couples are missing out on the untapped potential God designed for marital oneness that included mutual equality—intrinsically and functionally—and mutual authority. Limiting and restricting wives and women from using all the gifts God has given them results in such a loss. For example, many women who are celebrated as equals outside the church world have little, if any, interest in going to church. Women—especially younger women—who have been blessed with amazing gifts and have such kingdom advancing potential avoiding church because of gender restrictions is such a loss—and so sad. It also saddens us that many marriages and churches are missing out on the full potential in the functional equality the Apostle Paul spoke about when he wrote to the church in Galatia as he boldly declared that *both* men and women are equal and one in Christ Jesus [11].

"All that is to say, the good news for us is similar to other defining moments in church history such as the Protestant Reformation[12] and the abolition of slavery: as co-leadership and gender equality are embraced, we envision many positive results. The oneness Jesus spoke about in John 17—"so they may be one"—will become a powerful witness as men, women, and couples take the next steps in their spiritual formation individually and together. Unity will trump disunity, interdependence will replace independence, humility will replace hierarchy, and the kingdom of God will advance in amazing only-God ways."

CHAPTER 12

MARRIAGE IS NOT IT

Here we are, the last chapter. Then again, if you've been challenged to make some changes in your relationship to better **reflect** and **reveal** God's original co-leadership design for marriage, it could very well be the first chapter, the beginning of something new and beautiful between you and your spouse and God.

Looking back, we began this book with the following prayer, as you re-read it, **I.O.T.L.** *(inquire of the Lord)* as to how you can practically live it out.

> *May the God who is both great and good*
> *make your marriage stronger and your hearts braver.*
> *May He create not only a willingness to die for your marriage*
> *but also a passion to live for it.*

MARRIAGE IS NOT IT

We love marriage, but as much as we love marriage, we do not believe that marriage is it. Pause and slowly read these words out loud: *marriage is not it!* The Bible never suggests that marriage should be placed above the kingdom of God—"Seek first the kingdom of God," Jesus told us.[1] Focusing on marriage (or the family) should not be the main goal for fully devoted followers of Jesus Christ. Why? Because *marriage is not it.*

Marriage is defined by earthly limits: *till death do us part.* There will not be any marriages as we understand them in heaven. The Bible says, "At the resurrection people will neither marry nor be given in marriage."[2] Certainly marriage is high on God's list of priorities, but the goal of marriage should not be to focus solely on marriage.

In our lives, our personal kingdom assignment is marriage. However, our main message is not about marriage but about the Maker of marriage. There are only a few things that last forever: God, the kingdom of God, the Word of God, people's souls, and love. Therefore, as much as we love marriage, we understand that *marriage is not it.*

That being said, marriage is *something*, and hopefully we've shown in these pages what a wonderful something it is. As we finish up, here are a few what-if's followed by a dream.

WHAT IF?

The Bible declares, "Where there is no vision [revelation], the people perish."[3] Our humble sense is that we are on the verge of a powerful move of God that makes us wonder *what if?*

What if ...

God is allowing the cultural craziness, attempts to redefine marriage, and attacks on Christians in order to invite His followers to focus on **reflecting** and **revealing** God's plurality and goodness? This will ignite the synergistic power in love and truth as followers of Jesus Christ model the heart and love of a good God.

And what if the people of God redirected the attacks on marriage from those who misunderstand, misrepresent, or are trying to redefine marriage and focused on agreeing on absolutes? Pastor Rick Warren once said, "You can walk hand-in-hand without seeing eye-to-eye."[4] We wholeheartedly agree. Our encouragement to Christians is this: focus on what you are *for* rather than on what you are *against*. On a practical level, this begins by focusing on God and what He is for: God is pro-marriage, pro-intimacy, pro-unity, and pro-marital sex.

What if ...

God's original marriage principles of co-leadership in mutual equality and mutual authority were passionately reclaimed and humbly restored? If they were, it'd be a game changer. We believe marriage is the most untapped positive change agent in the world.

What if ...

When Jesus told His followers about the "greater things"[5] they would do, He was not referring to global evangelism, healings, demonic deliverance, and raising people from the dead? What if Jesus was describing a time when His followers would return to God's original co-leadership marriage principles?

What if ...

People with open hearts and minds pursue God as they humbly answer the question Jesus asked thousands of years ago and is still asking today: "Who do *you* say that I am?" We are not talking about any specific religion. One of our spiritual fathers says, "Is there truth in other religions? Yes. Is there beauty? Absolutely. Is there salvation—eternal life? The Bible states, 'There is no other Name in heaven or earth by which you can be saved.'"[6]

ARE YOU UP FOR A CHALLENGE?

We were members and lay leaders at Willow Creek Community Church for twenty years. Our pastor Bill Hybels and seasoned church leaders regularly challenged us to apply what we were learning—to not just be hearers but doers. We were taught that teaching and preaching should always lead to personal decisions and practical applications.

Following Willow Creek's example, we want to challenge each of you to review how you are currently living your marriage. Which view—male rulership, traditional-hierarchical-complementarian, egalitarian, or God's original co-leadership as we have presented it—best describes your current marriage relationship?

Are you up for a challenge? If so, agree for a period of time (say, three months) to give God's original co-leadership marriage principles a try. Practically implement the **Traffic Light Principle** decision-making model for all decisions. First, individually go to God— **I.O.T.L.** (*inquire of the Lord*)—and pour out your heart to Him. Ask for a red (*no*), yellow (*wait*), or green (*go*) light. Then bring what you sense from God to your spouse. Agree to exercise co-leadership by making decisions together in unity.

Practically, this involves making decisions only after you *both* have a green light.

After implementing this strategy, observe how you, your spouse, and your marriage advanced in spirit, soul, and body oneness. Specifically note the increased intimacy that co-leading in mutual equality and mutual authority provided.

Throughout this book we've shared many stories because we believe life revolves around story and stories build intimacy. However, the greatest story ever told is a story that is intimately connected to marriage. This story begins with a Triune God creating humankind—a man and a woman—in His image. They "became one" as husband and wife and together celebrated being "naked and not ashamed." Looking ahead, the greatest story ever told ends with a marriage, of Jesus returning to claim His bride, the church.

Marriage—is there another word that has such life-giving potential?

WE *DREAM* AND *IMAGINE* ABOUT GOD AND MARRIAGE

When it comes to God and marriage, we eagerly anticipate the next chapters in God's ongoing story. Over the years we've met people—especially more religious-orientated folks—who resist the game-changing co-leadership marriage message that was originally conceived in the heart of a never-changing God. They quickly dismiss returning to the principles of Paradise. We have other friends who say we are dreamers—and that may be true. But as we talk with couples, especially younger couples, about co-leadership in marriage, they are quick to become dreamers too.

We have a dream ...

We envision God using marriage and the power of story to engage our culture. We are not talking about a story centered on religious terminology or to-do lists. Rather, we are talking about men and women living in a Larger Story with God as the main character. We envision God using marriage to tell a story that draws people to Himself and opens the door for increased intimacy in all our relationships.

We have a dream ...

That followers of Christ will join together in unity and step into their call to be light and salt in the world. In our culture, as the pendulum continues to swing away from God's original design, this will create opportunities for the church to shine. Remember, the church is the prototype that is supposed to foreshadow the fullness of the kingdom of God. We see God inviting His church—the bride of Christ—to step into its finest hour as God's original co-leadership marriage principles are reclaimed. This will open the door for unbelievers to be drawn to investigate the newfound unity, celebration of diversity, and culture of community modeled within marriage and various communities of faith.

We have a dream ...

Of couples passionately and humbly embracing God's original co-leadership design. And the love Christian married couples model will speak volumes to a fatherless and motherless generation. We envision revival starting in the home as the Holy Spirit restores the hearts of fathers and mothers to their children and the hearts of children to their mothers and fathers.[7] We envision the millennial generation passionately embracing God's original co-leadership principles as they become models of a radical *togetherness*. This will open the door for God to birth networks of relationships united in heart about a marriage mission—*co-leadership*—that matters.

We have a dream ...

Of God inviting ordinary men and women to be the kindling that will ignite a marriage reformation. A reformation not focused on marriage preferences but on marriage absolutes; a reformation not focused on prevention but on redemption; a reformation not focused on specific goals and actions but on a loving Trinitarian God. A reformation that begins in the hearts of people who recognize and repent of pride, control, rebellion, and selfishness.

God is love, and He designed marriage with a specific mission—what we refer to as the **4 R's**. A man and woman enter into covenant with God and each other. They become one, and together:

> **Reflect and Reveal**: God's plurality and nature; mutual equality; *both* made in God's image
>
> **Rule**: co-lead *together*; mutual authority; *both* given the dominion (rulership) mandate
>
> **Reproduce**: be fruitful and multiply; *both* given the procreation mandate

Imagine the possibilities ...

Imagine a world where couples model the unity and community in God's Trinitarian nature.

Imagine a world where couples humbly live out the miracle and mystery of "two becoming one."

Imagine a world where couples walk together, passionate, naked, with no shame.

Imagine such a world, in all its breathtaking splendor.

We believe that world is possible.

But it must begin, one husband and wife, one couple at a time. As they …

> **I.O.T.L.** *(inquire of the Lord),*
> wait for His signal,
> then in unity go, hand in hand and side by side,
> as they step into that dream, that world—
> *together.*

EPILOGUE

If At First You Don't Succeed ...

Life Is Lived in a Story

tim+anne

Early on we described to you our first attempt to climb Pikes Peak. As beginners we envisioned ourselves conquering the mountain and standing on the summit, doing the happy dance. However, as you may recall, the day that began with such hope and excitement ended in frustration and disappointment.

Although our first attempt to reach the summit failed, we learned some important lessons and determined not to give up on our dream. The following month we gave it another try. Once again, we arrived at the trailhead before dawn. This time we made sure it was the correct trailhead. Although we were excited, we were less confident than before. Nevertheless, our excitement grew as we hit every checkpoint on our way up the trail.

Throughout our hike we noticed small rock piles—cairns—at regular intervals along the trail. Traditionally, as hikers continue along the trail, they add a stone to the growing pile of rocks. These small rock formations are like visual road maps that help other hikers stay on course and successfully reach their destination. Cairns also are used to commemorate important events. They are built on battlefields as memorials, on graves to honor the dead, and as standing stones after encounters with God.

Cairns are found on every continent of the world. Some of these mini-monuments are stacked so creatively that they would humble the most gifted designers and engineers. Each cairn tells a story and points the way.

Everything was going as planned on our second attempt to climb Pikes Peak. It was a beautiful day, and the trail was clearly marked. We reached the tree line and came to a clearing where we could see the summit. Our excitement increased as we continued hiking the switchbacks. A few more hours passed—and then suddenly our well-defined trail came to an abrupt end. We found ourselves standing before a massive pile of boulders that had to be twenty stories high.

Looking up, our first thought was *there is no way we will ever be able to make it to the top.* About that time, we noticed two hikers descending from the summit. Tim shouted out to them, "What's the best way to the top?" Pointing to a distant cairn stacked on top of a huge boulder, they shouted back, "Head toward that cairn. Then look for the next one. They will lead you to the top of the mountain."

Following their advice, we began our scramble up the rocks. We traversed back and forth up the mountain from one cairn to the next. But at some point all the rocks seemed to blend together. We found ourselves standing side by side on a huge boulder at almost fourteen thousand feet above sea level. We looked around in every direction, but there were no cairns in sight.

Although we were not sure of our next steps, we were certain of two things: First, we knew there had to be a way. Second, we knew other hikers had gone before us and successfully made it to the summit. Their success gave us the confidence to keep going.

Standing on that massive boulder we had a decision to make. *Together* we decided to **I.O.T.L.** and implement the **Traffic Light Principle**. *Together* we reached agreement in *unity* on which way to go. We took a deep breath and stepped out in faith. To our amazement, within a few steps, a cairn came into view. It was a spiritual experience for us. As we trusted God and stepped out in unity, God revealed the next cairn. Before long we reached the 14,115-foot summit. Standing on the top of Pikes Peak, we celebrated our accomplishment by doing the happy dance.

Together

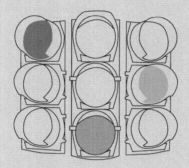

FURTHER STUDY

If you wish to find the specific places in the text with which these different sections correlate, please refer to the chapter listed in parenthesis or in the Notes section.

1. **Equality and Mutuality** (chapter 2, note 9)
2. **Hierarchy in the Trinity of God** (chapter 2, note 14)
3. **Different Genesis Accounts** (chapter 3, note 1)
4. **Gender Equality** (chapter 3, note 8)
5. **Man Naming the Woman** (chapter 3, note 12)
6. **God Speaking to the Man First** (chapter 4, note 20)
7. **Returning to Eden** (chapter 4, note 26)
8. **Treatment of Women** (chapter 6, note 8
9. **Theology** (chapter 8, note 8)
10. **Biblical Method of Interpretation** (chapter 8, note 10)
11. **Authority** (chapter 9, note 19)
12. **Jesus–the Quintessential Servant Leader** (chapter 10, note 23)
13. **Slavery** (chapter 11, note 9)
14. **Protestant Reformation** (chapter 11, note 11)

1. Equality and Mutuality
(chapter 2, note 9)

In his book *Beyond Sex Roles*, Dr. Gilbert Bilezikian emphasized the equality and mutuality God designed for one man and one woman in His original marriage design:

> The biblical text describes hierarchical organization as an element intrinsic to creation. But nowhere is it stated that man was intended to rule over woman within God's creation design. The fact that not a single reference, not a hint, not a whisper is made regarding authority roles between man and woman in a text otherwise permeated with hierarchical organization indicates that their relationship was one of nonhierarchical mutuality. Considerations of supremacy or leadership of one over the other were alien to the text and may not be imposed on it without violating God's original design for human relations.[1]

2. Hierarchy in the Trinity of God
(chapter 2, note 14)

We understand there are people who believe an authority structure exists within the Trinity of God. They believe God the Father has authority over God the Son and God the Holy Spirit. The majority of their argument, often referred to as Eternal Functional Subordinationism, focuses on God the Son—Jesus Christ—taking on human form and submitting to God the Father.

It's true: Jesus did submit to God the Father. But this occurred only after Jesus took on humanness in the incarnation. *Incarnation* is defined as

"God taking on human form as Jesus Christ."[2] Of course, Jesus in human form submitted to God the Father. But there is no evidence of hierarchy, headship, or subordination within the Trinity before the fall. That's because oneness, equality, unity, and community are intrinsic characteristics of the Godhead.

Others try to build a case for a hierarchy within the Trinity of God with what they refer to as ontological equality. Similar to Eternal Functional Subordinationism ontological equality proponents do not limit the kenosis to Jesus's redemptive ministry. *Kenosis* is defined as "Jesus Christ's act of partly giving up His divine status in order to become a man, as recorded in Philippians 2:6–7."[3] Ontological equality proponents extend this to Jesus's whole eternal state—they make it ontological. *Ontology* means "theory of existence."[4] In regard to Christ's kenosis, we agree with the traditional theological position of early church fathers. They believed that Jesus gave up the prerogatives of full equality with God. Therefore, Jesus coming to earth and being subordinate to the Father was not an eternal status. It began and is confined to his incarnation alone.

Eternal Functional Subordinationism and ontological equality can open the door to tri-theism, or having multiple gods. This was declared heresy in the early years of the church. Church leaders established creeds (e.g., the Apostles' Creed and the Nicene Creed) that stated church non-negotiable absolutes. These creeds stood decisively against hierarchy and subordination within the Trinity. They declared that God is both one and three in one. More recently the Evangelical Theological Society (ETS) affirmed this position as a part of its doctrinal basis; "God is a Trinity, Father, Son, and Holy Spirit, each an uncreated person, one in essence, equal in power and glory."[5] Any authority structure, hierarchy, or subordination within the Trinity of God violates the very nature of God.

3. Different Genesis Accounts
(chapter 3, note 1)

We understand there are a number of views and opinions surrounding the different creation accounts in Genesis. Some say they are historical; others say they are allegory, almost fable-like. We asked a veteran theologian to comment on the two accounts of creation in Genesis:

> I always thought that the purpose of Gen 1–2 was to provide the narrative as the vehicle for the revelation of basic truths such as the nature of God, his relation to the universe, to the earth and particularly to humans, humans to each other and the purposes of God for humankind. The fact that the creation order is not the same in Genesis 1 as in Genesis 2 indicates that the theology of the two creation accounts is more important than their discordant chronologies.[6]

4. Gender Equality
(chapter 3, note 8)

Philip B. Payne listed twenty statements in *Man and Woman, One in Christ* that depict the equality of man and woman in the pre-fall account in Genesis:

1. God creates both male and female in God's image and likeness (1:26–27; cf. 5:1–2).
2. God gives both male and female rule over the animals and all the earth (1:26b, 28).
3. God gives both male and female the same blessing and tells them together to be fruitful and increase in number, fill the earth, and subdue it (1:28–29; cf. 5:2).

4. God speaks directly to both the man and woman (1;28–29 "to them," "to you" plural twice).
5. God gives male and female together all plants for food (1:29 "to you" plural).
6. Woman is a "help" to man, a noun the OT never elsewhere uses of a subordinate (2:18, 20)
7. Woman "corresponds to" man, literally "in front of" man, face-to-face, not below (2:18, 20).
8. God makes woman from the man's rib, so she is made of the same substance as he (2:21–23).
9. The man recognizes, "This is now bone of my bones and flesh of my flesh" (2:23).
10. "Father and mother" are identified without hierarchical distinction (2:24).
11. A man is "united" to his wife, implying oneness (2:24).
12. A man becomes "one flesh" with his wife, implying unity (2:24).
13. Both the man and woman are naked and feel no shame, sharing moral sensibility (2:25).
14. The woman and the man are together at the temptation and fall (3:6); both faced temptation.
15. Both the woman and man eat the forbidden fruit (3:6), both exercising a (bad) moral choice.
16. The eyes of both are opened, they realize they are naked, and sew coverings (3:7).
17. Both hide from God (3:8), showing they both experience guilt.
18. God addresses both directly (3:9–13, 16–19), showing both have access to God.
19. Both pass blame (3:12–13), showing both have weakness.
20. God announces to both specific consequences to their sin (3:16–19); both are responsible.[7]

5. Man Naming the Woman
(chapter 3, note 12)

There are proponents of male hierarchy and female subordination who try to build a case against mutual equality and mutual authority in God's original marriage design based on man naming animals and their interpretation that man named the woman.

Yes, the man named the animals—but why? The purpose for naming the animals was for the man to find "a helper suitable for him."[8] Man naming the animals had nothing to do with him having any measure of authority over the woman. Giving a name does not equal having authority. In fact, in the Old Testament, there are twenty-five times women named children compared to twenty times when men named children.[9] The Old Testament involved a season of history where the male rulership marriage view—the husband ruling over his wife—was widespread. Women were treated as property and ruled by their husbands.

Therefore, the fact that women in the Old Testament named children more often than men had nothing to do with women having any measure of authority over men. Likewise, in the creation story the man naming the animals had nothing to do with any special measure of authority, leadership, or hierarchical priority. Remember, when the man named the animals, the woman was not even created yet.

But what about the man naming the woman? Let's review the text. When God created *man* the text reads, "God formed *man.*"[10] *Man* was God's designation for the human being He created. Likewise in Genesis 2:22 the text says, "And the LORD God fashioned into a *woman* the rib which He had taken from the man, and brought her to the man." *Woman* was God's designation for the female human being He created and brought to the man. Genesis 2:23 reads, "And the man said, "This is now bone of my bones, and flesh of my flesh; she shall be called *Woman*." *Woman* was God's designation in the preceding verse.

6. God Speaking to the Man First
(chapter 4, note 20)

There are those who suggest that because God spoke to the man first, this implies a hierarchy or some measure of male authority. However, for us that seems to be reading into the text. Couldn't it be possible that God approached the man first because He created man first, or because He gave the prohibition not to eat from the tree to the man before the woman was created?

Nevertheless, even though it is not stated anywhere in the text, if God speaking to the man first does represent some measure of authority, then shouldn't that position be applied consistently throughout Scripture? For example, after Jesus's resurrection, He spoke to a woman first. Therefore, to be fair and consistent, if the man in Eden had authority over women because God spoke to him first, then post-resurrection women should have authority over men since God spoke to a woman first after the resurrection.

For a person to build a doctrine of hierarchy and male authority simply because God spoke to the man before He spoke to the woman seems to be a colossal interpretative stretch.

7. Returning to Eden
(chapter 4, note 26)

Over the years when we teach about returning to Eden and God's original marriage principles, people challenge us, saying, "It's impossible for a person to return to Eden!" We agree—the Bible says the man and woman were driven out of Eden and God placed an angel and a flaming sword to keep humankind from returning.[11] However, when we encourage couples to return to Eden, we are speaking figuratively—"not literal, representational, representing by allegorical figures."[12]

Figurative language is used throughout the Bible. For example, Jesus spoke figuratively in Matthew 18 when He challenged people to become childlike so they could enter the kingdom of heaven. Obviously the people He was speaking to could not physically return to childhood. But Jesus, figuratively speaking, challenged people to return to the unconditional love, innocence, purity, and passion of a child. In fact, in the very next verse.[13] Jesus stated that the person who becomes childlike (not childish) and humbles himself as a child will be the greatest in the kingdom of heaven. Certainly Jesus did not expect people to return to childhood—but to reclaim the *principles* of childhood.

Likewise, we take the same position on marriage. We totally get that a person cannot physically return to Eden. We're not saying people need to walk around naked and only eat food from trees. But we believe a husband and wife can return to the marriage *principles* of Eden, which include mutual equality, mutual authority, and *togetherness* in co-leadership.

8. Treatment of Women
(chapter 6, note 8)

Jesus engaged with women in amazing ways. He traveled with women and they sat at His feet. He healed women and honored a woman who worshipped Him as she washed and anointed His feet with a year's wages of expensive perfume. Jesus's treatment of women was culture-shattering. In fact, the first person to tell others who Jesus really was—the Son of God—and the first person to see the resurrected Christ were women.

In addition, the apostle Paul respected and honored many women. He did not treat them as subordinates to men but as colaborers for the Lord. Review Paul's greetings to specific people at the conclusion of his letter to the church in Rome.[14] He commended Phoebe—a woman—and instructed the church to receive her in the Lord in a way worthy of the saints and to give her support as a leader in whatever matters she may need.[15] It's interesting to note that some Bible translations soften the title *deacon* when addressing Phoebe and instead translate *deacon* as *servant*.[16] But when the exact same word is used for men, translators use the title *deacon* or *minister*.[17]

Makes us wonder—*could the Enemy and traditional male patriarchy be in play somehow in the ways male translators wrote about women?*

At the end of Paul's letter to the church in Rome, he commended a number of early church leaders. The majority of colaborers the apostle Paul recognized and honored were women. For example, a woman named Junias is described as being "outstanding among the apostles."[18] Rachel Held Evans wrote,

As we've seen with Junia, some scholars will go to great lengths to work around a word or a phrase ... that doesn't fit with certain theological presuppositions. ("...'outstanding among the apostles' must really mean 'well known among the apostles.'" "'Well known among the apostles' [probably] means 'messenger.'").... **Like it or not, we bring ourselves and our biases to every translation and every reading of the text.**[19]

Review the life and ministry of Jesus. He came to earth, reclaimed dominion, and treated women with equality, dignity, and respect. This is totally in line with the equality and co-leadership that the man and woman enjoyed together before sin.

9. Theology
(chapter 8, note 8)

The term *theology* is not in the Bible. Theology is a human attempt to explain God's word and works in a reasonable and systematic way. Our personal experience is often that the people arguing about theology tend to be more religious-oriented people who have acquired lots of knowledge.

The apostle Paul warned that "knowledge puffs up and love builds up."[20] Knowledge is "general awareness or possession of information, facts, ideas, truths, or principles."[21]

The truth is that no matter how much knowledge a person has, there is no such thing as an infallible biblical interpreter. Remember, the Bible is not God. Jesus the Logos—the Word—is God, and the reality is that certain passages will continue to be debated until Jesus returns.

10. Biblical Method of Interpretation
(chapter 8, note 10)

Years ago we audited a course at Wheaton College.[22] Our professor, Dr. Gilbert Bilezikian, taught us a hermeneutical approach to interpreting the Bible that has served us well for decades. He divided history eschatologically into different seasons: creation, fall, redemption, and Christ's return. Creation was God's original design for humankind. The fall occurred after sin entered the story and resulted in many disastrous consequences. Jesus Christ's life, death, and life-giving resurrection brought redemption. And at some point in the future Jesus Christ will return and set up His kingdom on earth.

In addition, Dr. Bilezikian taught us to prayerfully marinate in the Scripture when attempting to discern the specific meaning of a biblical text and to ask the Holy Spirit for discernment. Practically, we filter the text through three specific components: *testamental*, *thematic*, and *hapax*. First, *testamental*: this means that, apart from creation, the New Testament takes precedence over the Old Testament. Second, *thematic*: the thematic principle means interpreting a text in the context of one theme at a time in one book at a time; don't cross-reference specific passages from book to book. Third, *hapax*: a hapax is something that occurs only one time. We were taught to be cautious not to base our theology solely on a hapax.

This method of biblical interpretation has been pure gold to us. We utilize these steps and prayerfully approach issues to see if they contradict the *principles* in the Bible. For example, youth ministry, Sunday worship, the sinner's prayer, the Holy Trinity, and the concept of a personal relationship with Jesus are not specifically stated in the Bible, but they do not violate any biblical *principles*; therefore we support all of these.

11. Authority
(chapter 9, note 19)

Philip Payne commented on marital authority in 1 Corinthians:

> The strikingly egalitarian understanding of the dynam-
> ics of marital relations expressed in Paul's symmetry
> throughout this passage is without parallel in the litera-
> ture of the ancient world.... Against a cultural backdrop
> where men were viewed as possessing their wives, Paul
> states in 7:2, "let each woman have her own husband."
> Against a cultural backdrop where women were viewed
> as owing sexual duty to their husbands, Paul states in 7:3,
> "Let the husband fulfill his marital duty to his wife."
>
> It is hard to imagine how revolutionary it was for Paul
> to write in 1 Corinthians 7:4, "the husband does not have
> authority over his own body, but his wife does."[23]

12. Jesus–the Quintessential Servant Leader
(chapter 10, note 23)

Bill Hybels commented on Jesus as a leader:

> Hand down, the single most impressive leader in the his-
> tory of the world is Jesus of Nazareth...the facts speak
> for themselves. No leader ever cast a more expansive or
> breathtaking vision—nothing less than the redemption of
> the planet—than did Jesus Christ. No leader ever built a
> higher-impact team in a shorter period of time with less
> talent to work with. No leader ever instilled deeper values

or inspired people more than Jesus Christ—in many cases, enough for them to die for the cause.

Certainly, no leader has ever changed the course of human history the way Jesus did...and is still doing, more than two-thousand years later.

I'd say it all adds up to some pretty compelling leadership evidence: He was the best leader ever.[24]

13. Slavery
(chapter 11, note 9)

The following is a Presbyterian resolution from the mid-1800s. For centuries, church leaders used a handful of biblical texts to justify slavery.

> Resolved:—"That slavery has existed from the days of those good old slave-holders and patriarchs, Abraham, Isaac, and Jacob, (who are now in the kingdom of heaven,) to the time when the apostle Paul sent a run-away home to his master, Philemon, and wrote a christian and fraternal letter to this slave-holder, which we find still stands in the canon of the Scriptures—and that slavery has existed ever since the days of the apostle, and does now exist." ...
> Resolved:—"That as the relative duties of master and slave are taught in the scriptures, in the same manner as those of parent and child, and husband and wife, the existence of slavery itself is not opposed to the will of God; and whoever has a conscience too tender to recognize this relation as lawful, is 'righteous over much,' is 'wise above what is written,' and has submitted his neck to the

yoke of men, sacrificed his christian liberty of conscience, and leaves the infallible word of God for the fancies and doctrines of men."[25]

Sad to say, but when we review conversations on the blogosphere surrounding gender and the idea that men and women are equal intrinsically and functionally, at times the conversation can sound similar to the judgmental responses about slavery, as illustrated above. Our prayer is that men and women will humbly revisit marriage and gender texts as they recognize and respect each other and differing interpretations.

14. Protestant Reformation
(chapter 11, note 11)

Throughout history the church has experienced many adjustments in its theology and teachings. The Bible is filled with seasons of history where God spoke, and seasons where He appeared to be silent. And throughout history we see God intervening. For example, shortly after Jesus's resurrection, the church was birthed. The early church was not a specific denomination but represented all followers of Jesus Christ. The marching orders for Christ followers included the Great Commandment (*love*) and the Great Commission (*go*). Men and women left the familiarity and comforts of their religious heritage to spread the good news that forgiveness for sins and an intimate relationship with God were now possible. This radical shift involved the message *repent*. Both women and men repented (turned away from sin), received Jesus, and were baptized (in water and the Holy Spirit). The church flourished, and countless lives and eternities were impacted.

However, after a number of generations, God's simple Holy Spirit–led plan of salvation by faith was replaced with salvation by works. The life-giving culture of church unity and community was replaced by a culture of leadership and hierarchy. This new corporate church culture became corrupt and self-focused. One of the results was that church leaders sold indulgences: "Remission of punishment for sin—in Roman Catholicism, a granting by the pope of partial remission of time to be spent in purgatory or of some other consequence of sin. In the Middle Ages, a practice of selling indulgences grew up as payment for sins."[26]

But God still speaks ... and in His appointed time, everything changed. In the early fifteenth century, the Holy Spirit spoke to a Roman Catholic leader named Martin Luther. Luther received fresh revelation while studying the Bible. He realized what was lost: the simple good news of the gospel message. He reclaimed what was stolen by corrupt church leaders—God's plan of salvation. And at the risk of personal harm and excommunication, he encouraged people to turn away from a gospel of works and to embrace a gospel of salvation by grace through faith. His mantra was the just shall live by faith. He was interrogated, intimidated, and threatened by church leaders who demanded he recant what he said. He responded, "Here I stand. I can do no other."

ADDITIONAL CHALLENGE

Thank you for investing in reading our book. Our prayer is that God builds a co-leadership marriage team, a network of relationships united in heart about a mission—God and marriage—that matters.

We challenge those interested in marriage and gender issues to invest in further study. First **I.O.T.L.** *(inquire of the Lord)*, and invite the Holy Spirit to guide you. John 16:13 says; "When the Holy Spirit, who is truth, comes, he shall guide you into all truth... (TLB)". We suggest you begin with the Bible: start in Genesis 1:1—"In the beginning." Ask God to help you envision what His original design for marriage was like *before* sin entered the marriage story. Compare the mutual equality and mutual authority—co-leadership—in God's original marriage design to later spawned marriage views that included hierarchy, male authority, and female subordination.

As far as later marriage views, countless sermons have been preached, and numerous books and blogs written about equality, headship, submission, and authority. We prayerfully chose to invest only one chapter on these topics. Instead, our primary focus was on God's original marriage design. Nevertheless, for those wanting to explore perspectives that align with male rulership and traditional-hierarchical-complementarian marriage views. A website that provides scholarly information, free articles, book reviews, and a blog from traditional-complementarian gender and marriage perspectives is the Council for Biblical Manhood and Womenhood

(CBMW) at http://cbmw.org/. Key CBMW proponents include Wayne Grudem, John Piper, Owen Strachan, John MacArthur, and Mark Driscoll.

For an excellent egalitarian presentation about gender, read "A Challenge for Proponents of Female Subordination to Prove Their Case from the Bible" by Dr. Gilbert Bilezikian. He wrote,

> The purpose of this challenge is to prompt Christians to grapple with biblical facts rather than to accept traditional assumptions about female roles. What is at stake is not the role of women as much as the definition of the church as authentic biblical community. Is it possible for a local church to aspire to define itself as biblical community when more than half its constituency is excluded from participating in the most significant aspects of its life?[1]

His full challenge can be found at http://www.cbeinternational.org/?q=content/challenge-proponents-female-submission-prove-their-case-bible. Dr. Bilezikian's book *Beyond Sex Roles* is a classic.

A website that provides scholarly information, free articles, book reviews, and a blog from an egalitarian perspective is Christians for Biblical Equality (CBE) at http://www.cbeinternational.org/. Key CBE proponents include Gilbert Bilezikian, Mimi Haddad, Carolyn Custis James, Philip B. Payne, and Rachel Held Evans.

We bless your journey and your pursuit of God's truths, specifically truths surrounding His original marriage design. Similar to believers in other epochal seasons in church history (such as the Protestant Reformation and the abolition of slavery), we believe God still speaks. The Bible reminds us, "We know in part,"[2] and we sense God is getting ready to do a celestial reboot as He provides fresh revelation about togetherness in mutual equality and mutual authority—what we call co-leadership.

Unity will trump disunity; interdependence will replace independence; mutual equality will replace functional inequality, humility will replace hierarchy; and God's kingdom will advance. As Jesus said when He spoke about marriage, "what God has joined **together**, let no one separate."[3] Our prayer is those who have ears to hear—with open minds and teachable hearts—**I.O.T.L.** as they humbly revisit marriage *in the beginning*.

ACKNOWLEDGMENTS

Life is lived in a story, and writing this book has been a story filled with family and friends. Our experience is that anything successful in life involves a team. God built an amazing team for this project. The reality is there are too many team members to list. Nevertheless, we want to extend our heartfelt thanks to the following people:

+ To our Prayer Shield Team, who pray for us, our marriage, family, and ministry—and for marriage reformation. Your encouragement, passion for prayer, and commitment to kingdom advancement goes before us and opens the door for God's truth to penetrate hearts.

+ To our parents, Bill and Jeanne Evans and Jack and Pat O'Shaughnessy, for laying a strong foundation that continues to be built on.

+ To our children: Tim, Amy and Curt, Colleen and Johnny, and Cate. A long time ago, God invited us to join Him on a journey. He wanted to tell a story through our lives. As a family we all agreed to take a leap of faith, believing the net would appear. Every chapter of our story has been a mix of adventure and challenge. As your parents, we want to thank you for being willing to follow God even when it cost you something. Thank you for choosing the Larger Story and learning earlier than most kids do that "it's not about me."

+ To our grandchildren: Joel, Trey, Grace, Emma, Jack ... and future grand-kids (and great-grandkids). Our thanks flows out of who you are, rather than anything you've done. Your sheer existence brings us indescribable joy!

+ To spiritual parents. Dick and Alice Swetman, you introduced us to a personal relationship with Jesus and imparted to us a passion for God and His Word. Thank you for loving and praying for our clan. To Gilbert Bilezikian—in the mid-1980s we took your course at Wheaton College, where we were introduced to many of the principles in this book. Gil, your course was life-changing. Thank you for encouraging us to pursue biblical community and passionately live out spirit-soul-body oneness. To Chief Peter and Doris Wagner for encouraging us to have a prayer shield team, and challenging us to make walking in humility (by God's grace) a top life priority. And to Bill and Lynne Hybels, our twenty years under your leadership at Willow Creek was foundational to who we are today. Thank you to all the mentors, spiritual parents, and pastors God has blessed us with over the years; the list is too long to type.

+ To key REAL LIFE friends and partners: Jim and Kathy Kubik, Keith and Robyn Brodie, TJ and Deb Bratt, John and Therese Tekautz, Stephanie and Jay Frankhouse, Steve and Pam DeBoer, George and Melodee Cook, Jared and Megan Anderson, Ruth and Alan Breuker, Paul and Barb Osburn, John and Caryl O'Shaughnessy, Justin and Valerie Ensor, and many oth-ers. Your prayers, partnership, and belief in us have been like a drink from a fire hydrant.

+ Thank you to Ken Gire; you walked with us on this project from day one and provided much-needed wisdom and encouragement (you continue to be our favorite author). Thank you, Don Pape—your experience, sense of humor, and encouragement throughout this process was so life giving.

To our editors: John Blase, thank you for your friendship, love of words, and ongoing encouragement. And Caitlyn Carlson—your enthusiasm for getting things perfect and your attention to detail are beyond amazing. To Amy Konyndyk, our cover designer and interior-layout expert extraordinaire. To Laura Dobson for the book back cover picture. And to Brad Herman: your passion for books inspires us. You *all* became key partners in the completion of this project.

+ While writing this book, we were blessed to be on the receiving end of encouraging words and timely support that cheered us on to press in and keep going. Special thanks to super encouragers Amy and Curt DeBoer, and Gilbert Bilezikian. And to Tim Jr. and Cate Evans, Colleen and John Stickl, Angela and Danny Gieck, Linda and Tim Laird, Leah and Matthew Tisthammer, Haley and Dave Wilson, John and Kem Stickl, Holly and Glenn Pakiam, Lynn and Jim Eichoff, Cherie and Morgan Snyder, Bruce and Sue Osterink, Kate and Troy DeWys, Tom and Jan Murray, Pearl and Vern Manuel, David and Kate Kubik, Jessica and Brad Sheasby, Marty and Marilyn O'Connor, Tom and Julie Vroon, Chuck and Bev Osterink, Jen and Ben Slenk, Barb and Bill Vroon, Tom and Marilyn Bratt, Denny and Scoob Ellens, Jack and Becky Sytsema, Ben and Lauretta Patterson, Mary and Mike Banas, Kathy and Mike Barry, Anne and Mike Risher, Jodi and Miles Anderson, Julynn and Doug Mullinix, Christine and David King, Paige and Jon Egan, Matthew and Tiffany Gowler, Mindy and Jordan Linscombe, Jason and Keely Cormier, Andy and Glorie Catarisanos, Becca and Stu Reynolds, Charles and Judy Cash, Dan and Jane Evans, Paul and Lori Byerly, John and Amy Dale, Chester and Betsy Kylstra, Edna Riley, Barry and Sandra Falkenstein, Rick and Michelle Hensley, Jim and Janice Watson, Phyllis and Dennis Scheminske, Scott and Theresa Beck, Jeffrey Youngbluth, Dick Savidge, Mike Ruman, Tom Stella, Liz Beyer, Ray Williams, Elizabeth Ross ... *and so many others*.

Thank you for your prayers, notes, calls, generosity, offers of places to write, feedback, and gestures of kindness that arrived at the perfect times.

+ Thank you to those who endorsed our book: Dr. Che and Sue Ahn, Jared and Megan Anderson, Dr. Gilbert Bilezikian, Dr. Timothy Brown, Jon and Paige Egan, Ken Gire, Dr. Mimi Haddad, Glenn and Holly Pakiam, Morgan and Cherie Snyder, John and Colleen Stickl, Jack and Becky Sytsema, and David and Haley Wilson.

+ A special thank-you to those who are represented (anonymously) through the REAL LIFE stories in this book and to the men and women in our marriage and co-leadership community small groups throughout the decades. Your lives tell a story that points us to God. Thank you for having the courage to share the joys and struggles of your journey with other travelers. Seeing you advance in intimacy with God, and watching married couples co-leading together, inspires us to stay on the trail.

+ We thank God for and we bless others who will build on what we have written about gender equality and co-leadership in marriage. Our prayer is that God builds a co-leadership marriage team, a network of relationships united in heart about a mission—God and marriage—that matters.

+ Lastly, we thank God for creating marriage, intimacy, and sexuality. It's our prayer that Your original together-ness in co-leadership marriage design is passionately reclaimed and humbly restored.

ABOUT THE AUTHORS

tim+anne evans are a real-life couple who love marriage. For thirty-eight years they have passionately explored the miracle and mystery of two becoming one in the context of God's original co-leadership marriage design. They are parents, grandparents, pastoral counselors, and spiritual parents. Tim is a retired fire chief; Anne is a licensed nurse and certified Life Purpose Coach. They are both ordained ministers, have master and doctor of practical ministry diplomas from Wagner Leadership Institute, and are nationally certified Healing House Network ministers. They enjoy their marriage, kids, and grandkids; friendships; hiking; motorcycling; and living in Colorado near Pikes Peak. *Together* they lead REAL LIFE Ministries full time.

Look for the upcoming *Together: Reclaiming Co-Leadership in Marriage Companion Journal*. This tool dovetails with this book and encourages individuals, couples, and small groups to explore co-leadership.

REAL LIFE MINISTRIES

+ REAL LIFE Ministry's mission is to help men, women, and couples advance in loving God, loving a spouse, loving others and growing in self love. (Matthew 22:37-40), through:

+ Marriage Advance Seminars (1-2-3 day gatherings)
+ Forgiveness workshop
+ Communication workshop
+ Overcoming Destructive Cycles workshop
+ Intimacy and Sexuality workshop
+ Marriage tune-ups
+ Marriage intensives
+ Pastoral counseling
+ Pre-marital counseling
+ Restoring the Foundations; www.restoringyourlife.org
+ Life coaching and life plans (anne);
   www.lifepurposecoachingcenters.com
+ Men's and Women's Advances

tim+anne evans

REAL LIFE ministries
www.RLmarriage.com
PO Box 6800
Colorado Springs, CO 80934

One last request regarding our vision quest of getting God's co-leadership marriage message out. Marketing and networking principles teach that word-of-mouth is the best way to promote a message. Would you please take a few minutes and help us promote our co-leadership message?

Go to Amazon, locate our "TOGETHER" book, hit LIKE, then make a COMMENT. Next, contact your friends and spheres of influence (personally and electronically) and recommend "TOGETHER."

Thank you for partnering with us.

To purchase additional print or ebooks visit Amazon.com

NOTES

Prologue

1. Proverbs 18:22
2. 1 Corinthians 7:28

Chapter 1: Unity Trumps Disunity

1. 1 Samuel 23:4, 2 Samuel 5:19, 1 Samuel 28:6, 2 Chronicles 1:5, Judges 20:27
2. James 1:5
3. James 1:5
4. James 1:5

Chapter 2: The Starting Place

1. Genesis 1:1–3 NIV
2. Genesis 1:2 NIV
3. John 1:1 NIV
4. John 1:14
5. Colossians 1:15–16
6. Genesis 1:26
7. *Encarta Dictionary*, s.v. "image"
8. *Encarta Dictionary*, s.v. "likeness"
9. See "Equality and Mutuality" in the Further Study section
10. Genesis 1:27
11. 2 Corinthians 1:3–4
12. 1 Thessalonians 2:7–8
13. 1 John 4:8
14. See "Hierarchy in the Trinity of God" in the Further Study section.
15. Genesis 1:26
16. Genesis 1:28b
17. Genesis 1:28
18. Genesis 1:28
19. Genesis 2:25
20. Ephesians 6:3

Chapter 3: From "Good" ... to "Not Good" ... to "Very Good"

1. See "Different Genesis Accounts" in the Further Study section.
2. Genesis 2:7
3. Genesis 2:15; in the original language, *man* is more accurately translated as *human*.
4. Genesis 2:18; in the original language, *man* is more accurately translated as *human*.
5. Genesis 2:18
6. Dr. Gilbert Bilezikian, *Beyond Sex Roles* (Grand Rapids: Baker Academic, 2006), 21–22.
7. Carolyn Custis James, *Half the Church* (Grand Rapids: Zondervan, 2010), 115–116.
8. See "Gender Equality" in the Further Study section.
9. Genesis 2:21–22
10. Genesis 2:7
11. Genesis 2:22
12. See "Man Naming the Woman" in the Further Study section.
13. Genesis 2:23
14. Ephesians 5:31 ASV
15. 1 Corinthians 4:15
16. 3 John 4
17. Genesis 2:25
18. John Blase, "The Beautiful Fall," Burnside Writers Collective, September 2, 2010, http://burnsidewriters.com/2010/09/02/the-beautiful-fall/. Used with permission.
19. Genesis 1:1
20. Genesis 1:27
21. The concept of Larger Story/smaller story living is adapted from the teaching and writing of John Eldredge and Dr. Dan B. Allender.
22. Romans 1:16
23. C. Peter Wagner, *Your Spiritual Gifts Can Help Your Church Grow* (Ventura, CA: Regal, 1974), 44.

Chapter 4: Co-leadership Lost

1. John 10:10
2. Genesis 2:16–17
3. Genesis 3:1
4. Genesis 3:2
5. Genesis 3:3
6. Genesis 3:4–5
7. Genesis 3:6
8. Genesis 3:5
9. Genesis 3:7
10. Genesis 3:4
11. Genesis 3:16
12. Genesis 3:16
13. Genesis 3:9
14. Genesis 3:10
15. Genesis 3:11

16. For excellent teaching on shame we recommend Dr. Brené Brown.

17. Sandra D. Wilson, *Released From Shame* (Downers Grove, IL: InterVarsity, 2002), 10.

18. Chester Kylstra, *Transforming Your Business* (Hendersonville, NC: Proclaiming His Word, 2006), 196.

19. Genesis 3:11–13

20. See "God Speaking to the Man First" in the Further Study section.

21. Genesis 3:16

22. Genesis 3:17–19

23. Dr. Gilbert Bilezikian, *Beyond Sex Roles* (Grand Rapids: Baker Academic, 2006), 42.

24. Genesis 3:12

25. Genesis 3:6

26. See "Returning to Eden" in the Further Study section.

Chapter 5: Co-leadership Regained

1. Luke 19:10

2. 1 John 3:8

3. Luke 19:10

4. Luke 4:18

5. Carolyn Custis James, *Half the Church* (Grand Rapids: Zondervan, 2010), 167.

6. Matthew 3:17

7. Matthew 4:3 NIV

8. Matthew 4:4 NIV

9. Matthew 4:6 NIV

10. Matthew 4:7 NIV

11. Watchman Nee, *The Finest of the Wheat: Volume 1* (New York: Christian Fellowship Publishers, 1992), 475–476.

12. Matthew 4:9 NIV

13. Matthew 4:10 NIV

14. Luke 4:13

15. Luke 19:10

16. Hebrews 9:16

17. Ecclesiastes 4:12 NIV

18. 1 Corinthians 7:28 NIV

19. Ephesians 5:21

20. Philippians 2:3

21. 1 Corinthians 7:4

22. Romans 6:14 NKJV

Chapter 6: Did Jesus Say Anything about Marriage?

1. Genesis 19:7–8
2. *Encarta Dictionary,* s.v. "misogyny."
3. *Encarta Dictionary*, s.v. "patriarchy."
4. Genesis 3:16
5. Matthew 19:3 NIV
6. Matthew 19:4–6 NIV
7. Matthew 19:10
8. See "Treatment of Women" in the Further Study section.
9. For information about the religious spirit, we recommend *Freedom from the Religious Spirit* by C. Peter Wagner.
10. Scot McKnight, "What Is the Gospel?" *Next-Wave*, December 2005, http://outwardthinking.com/thenextwave/archives/issue85/index-57618.cfm.html.
11. Genesis 1:28
12. Genesis 1:27
13. Matthew 22:37–40
14. 1 Corinthians 7:5
15. Song of Solomon 5:1
16. 2 Samuel 12:24
17. Hebrews 13:4 **ESV**
18. *Encarta Dictionary*, s.v. "honor."
19. *Encarta Dictionary,* s.v. "defiled."

Chapter 7: From "Me" to "We"

1. C. H. Spurgeon, "Things Unknown," March 4, 1900, http://www.spurgeon.org/sermons/2664.htm.
2. Dr. Gilbert Bilezikian, "Marriage and Family in the New Testament" (class, Wheaton College, spring 1987).
3. James 1:5
4. Erwin Raphael McManus, *Soul Cravings* (Nashville: Thomas Nelson, 2006), 8.
5. Hebrews 12:25
6. Richard J. Foster, *Celebration of Discipline* (New York: Harper Collins, 1978).
7. James 4:2b
8. Philippians 4:6
9. 2 Corinthians 10:5
10. 1 Corinthians 2:15 NASB
11. James 1:5
12. Proverbs 11:14
13. Colossians 3:17
14. Matthew 6:33
15. 1 Thessalonians 5:16–18
16. Philippians 4:7 ESV
17. Genesis 1–2
18. Luke 18:29–30
19. Ephesians 4:1 ESV
20. 2 Timothy 1:9

21. 1 Samuel 16:7 NIV
22. Luke 6:45
23. Matthew 22:36–40

Chapter 8: Absolutes versus Preferences

1. *Encarta Dictionary*, s.v. "absolute."
2. In recent years this debate has been rekindled. It's interesting to note that passionate people of faith are in different camps in the Calvinism-Arminianism debate. Godly Christ followers who prefer Calvinism include Charles Spurgeon, Benjamin Breckenridge Warfield, John McArthur, and John Piper. Godly Christ followers who prefer Arminianism include John Wesley, C. S. Lewis, Billy Graham, and Gilbert Bilezikian.
3. Matthew 6:33 ESV
4. Genesis 3:16
5. James 4:7–8
6. Romans 6:14 NKJV
7. 1 John 4:4
8. See "Theology" in the Further Study section.
9. John 16:7
10. See "Biblical Method of Interpretation" in the Further Study section.

Chapter 9: Equality—Headship—Submission—Authority

1. Dr. Gilbert Bilezikian, conversation and email to the authors, December 20, 2013.
2. Matthew 19:4–6
3. Ephesians 5:25a
4. Ephesians 5:25b
5. Ephesians 5:29
6. *Encarta Dictionary*, s.v. "impose."
7. 1 Timothy 2:5 NIV
8. Ephesians 5:1-2
9. Ephesians 5:3
10. Ephesians 5:4
11. Ephesians 5:5
12. Ephesians 5:6-7
13. Ephesians 5:8-14
14. Ephesians 5:15-17
15. Ephesians 5:18
16. Ephesians 5:19
17. Ephesians 5:20
18. Ephesians 5:21
19. Ephesians 5:22 (NAS)
20. 1 Peter 3:1

21. Ephesians 5:21
22. 1 Peter 3:1
23. 1 Peter 3:7
24. 1 Peter 5:12
25. John 13:34
26. Ephesians 5:21
27. 1 Corinthians 7
28. Ephesians 6:1
29. Ephesians 5:21
30. Ephesians 5:31 ASV
31. Ephesians 5:18, 21
32. Ephesians 5:22–23
33. Dr. Gilbert Bilezikian, *Beyond Sex Roles* (Grand Rapids: Baker Academic, 2006)
34. Genesis 21:12
35. See "Authority" in the Further Study section.
36. 1 Corinthians 13
37. Ephesians 5

Chapter 10: Love—Respect—Roles

1. 1 Timothy 2:11
2. 1 Timothy 2:12
3. 1Timothy 2:12
4. 1 Timothy 2:9
5. 1 Timothy 2:8
6. 1 Corinthians 11:5
7. Romans 16
8. Romans 16:1
9. Romans 16:3
10. Romans 16:6
11. Romans 16:7
12. Titus 1:10–11
13. Romans 16:16; 1 Corinthians 16:20; 1 Thessalonians 5:26; 1 Peter 5:14
14. Matthew 22:37–40
15. 1 Corinthians 12:31 NIV
16. 1 Corinthians 13:13 NIV
17. Hebrews 13:4
18. John 21:15–17
19. *Encarta Dictionary*, s.v. "machismo."
20. John Blase, "Wishes," *The Beautiful Due*, May 4, 2013, http://thebeautifuldue.wordpress.com/2013/05/04/wishes/.
21. Galatians 3:26–28 NIV
22. Mimi Haddad, "Is God Male?: Part 4," *Arise*, May 17,2012, http://www.cbeinternational.org/?q=content/2012-5-17-god-male-part-4-arise-e-newsletter.
23. Matthew 16:24 See "Jesus—the Quintessential Servant Leader" in the Further Study section.
24. Hosea 11:9; Numbers 23:19

25. Exodus 15:3
26. 2 Corinthians 1:3–4
27. 1 Thessalonians 2:7–8

Chapter 11: Co-leadership Is Liberating for Everyone

1. Matthew 28:18 NIV
2. 1 Timothy 2:5 NIV; *mankind* in the original has been changed to *humankind*.
3. Ephesians 5:21
4. 1 Corinthians 7:4
5. Philippians 2:3
6. Genesis 3:16
7. Romans 4:2
8. John 16:13
9. See "Slavery" in the Further Study section.
10. Brené Brown, Global Leadership Summit at Willow Creek Church, August 2013.
11. Galatians 3:28
12. See "Protestant Reformation" in the Further Study section.

Chapter 12: Marriage Is Not "It"

1. Matthew 6:33 ESV
2. Matthew 22:30 NIV
3. Proverbs 29:18 KJV
4. Rick Warren, interview with Jack Tapper, *ABC This Week*, April 7, 2012, http://abcnews.go.com/blogs/politics/2012/04/rick-warren-coarsening-of-our-culture-concerns-me/.
5. John 14:12
6. Ben Patterson, "The Spirit Says Arise" (chapel message, Hope College Dimnent Memorial Chapel, Holland, MI, 1996–1997).
7. Luke 1:17

Further Study

1. Dr. Gilbert Bilezikian, conversation and email to the authors, December 20, 2013.
2. *Encarta Dictionary*, s.v. "incarnation."
3. *Encarta Dictionary*, s.v. "kenosis."
4. *Encarta Dictionary*, s.v. "ontology."
5. Evangelical Theological Society (ETS) Doctrinal Statement: "The Bible alone, and the Bible in its entirety, is the Word of God written and is therefore inerrant in the autographs. God is a Trinity, Father, Son, and Holy Spirit, each an uncreated person, one in essence, equal in power and glory." http://www.etsjets.org/
6. Dr. Gilbert Bilezikian, email to the authors, September 9, 2013.
7. Philip B. Payne, *Man and Woman, One in Christ* (Grand Rapids: Zondervan, 2009), 53–54.

8. Genesis 2:20

9. John Otwell, *And Sarah Laughed; the Status of Women in the Old Testament* (Philadelphia: Westminster, 1977), 112.

10. Genesis 2:7

11. Genesis 3:23–24

12. *Encarta Dictionary*, s.v. "figurative."

13. Matthew 18:4

14. Romans 16

15. Romans 16:2

16. Romans 16:1

17. Ephesians 6:21; Colossians 1:25; 4:7

18. Romans 16:7

19. Rachel Held Evans, "The Bibles We Read ..." Rachel Held Evans, http://rachelheldevans.com/blog/the-bibles-we-read.

20. 1 Corinthians 8:1 NIV

21. *Encarta Dictionary*, s.v. "knowledge."

22. Gilbert Bilezikian, *"Marriage and Family in the New Testament" (lecture, Wheaton College,* spring 1987).

23. Payne, *Man and Woman, One in Christ*, 106–107.

24. Bill Hybels, When Leadership and Discipleship Collide (Zondervan: Grand Rapids, 2007), 9.

25. *Pamphlets on Slavery: Volume 10* (London: J. Hatchard and Son, 1833), 30.

26. *Encarta Dictionary*, s.v. "indulgences."

Additional Challenge

1. Gilbert Bilezikian, "A Challenge for Proponents of Female Subordination To Prove Their Case from The Bible,"
http://www.cbeinternational.org/?q=content/challenge-proponents-female-submission-prove-their-case-bible

2. 1 Corinthians 13:9

3. Matthew 19:6 NIV